the EDIBLE RAINBOW GARDEN

Rosalind Creasy

PERIPLUS

First published in 2000 by
PERIPLUS EDITIONS (HK) LTD.,
with editorial offices at 153 Milk Street,
Boston, Massachusetts 02109 and
5 Little Road #08-01
Singapore 536983.

Library of Congress Cataloging-in-Publication Data
Creasy, Rosalind.
   The edible rainbow garden / Rosalind Creasy.—1st ed.
      p. cm.
   ISBN 962-593-299-2 (paper)
   1. Vegetables gardening. 2. Vegetables-Varieties.
   3. Cookery (Vegetables) I. Title.
SB321.C8247 2000
635--dc21   99-036395
                                                          CIP

                        Distributed by

USA   SOUTHEAST ASIA
Tuttle Publishing   Berkeley Books Pte. Ltd.
Distribution Center   5 Little Road #08-01
Airport Industrial Park   Singapore 536983
364 Innovation Drive   Tel: (65) 280-3320
North Clarendon, VT 05759   Fax: (65) 280-6290
Tel: (802) 773-8930
Tel: (800) 526-2778
                                 JAPAN
                                 Tuttle Publishing
CANADA   RK Building, 2nd Floor
Raincoast Books   2-13-10 Shimo-Meguro
8680 Cambie Street   Meguro-Ku
Vancouver, Canada V6P 6M9   Tokyo, 153, Japan
Tel: (604) 323-7100   Tel: (813) 5437-6171
Fax: (604) 323-2600   Fax: (813) 5437-0755

First edition
05 04 03 02 01 00
10 9 8 7 6 5 4 3 2 1

Design by Kathryn Sky-Peck

PRINTED IN SINGAPORE

contents

the edible rainbow garden

I LOVE BRIGHT COLORS! My dresses are red, bright blue, even deep purple. My house is decorated with primary colors, and sometimes you practically need sunglasses to look at my garden. I dream in Technicolor. While I thrill to Ansel Adams's black-and-white photographs, I photograph in color only. Intellectually I realize that not everyone feels the way I do about color. I tell myself there are people who love beige and others who decorate solely with black and white, but in my heart I'm not sure these people really exist.

Given my predilection for colors, it's not surprising that I'm enamored with colorful vegetables. Why grow only standard green kale or broccoli when I can have purple ones too?—providing, of course, that they taste good. Why

limit myself to green bell peppers when I can have yellow, orange, and violet varieties as well? It's not the colors alone that I glory in; it's the infinite variety that nature offers. Just as I delight in seeing exotic birds and insects and growing unfamiliar species of flowers, so I enjoy growing and cooking with vegetables of unusual colors. I love putting my hands on

them and sharing them with others. When a neighbor's child helps me harvest blue potatoes, we take pleasure in the color together. I get a kick out of serving pink scallions or thinly sliced raw purple artichokes to a visiting gardener. All in all, color is a whole dimension of my edible garden to experiment with and enjoy.

I can trace my fascination with colorful vegetables back twenty years to my discovery of orange tomatoes and purple string beans. These vegetables were so much fun I started looking for other varieties in unusual colors. At first, my collection built slowly. In those "monochromatic days," most people thought it quite odd to grow or eat vegetables in colors they had not grown up with. And few colorful varieties were offered. Before long I met Jan Blüm, fellow color enthusiast and owner of Seeds Blüm, and we started playing that great gardening game, "Have I Got Something for You!" I'd

Why plant only the standard colors of vegetables? Why not plant a harvest of unusual vegetables *(opposite)* that includes 'Yellow Doll' watermelon, 'Plum Purple' radishes, 'Cherokee Purple' tomato, 'Lemon' cucumbers, 'Asian Bride' eggplant, and 'French White' zucchini.

show her lavender eggplants and she'd tell me about yellow peas and red celery. I'd describe chartreuse broccoli and she'd present me with red orach and green radishes. I always felt on the cutting edge with my vegetables, but I was constantly outclassed! Jan had an advantage. She worked with people who sought and saved heirloom vegetables—many of which were very colorful. These heirloom gardeners were dedicated to preserving an eroding gene pool, which was a much more serious reason to be passionate about unusual varieties.

Given the extra energy from dedicated heirloom gardeners and the awakening interest among savvy chefs who saw the culinary potential, colorful vegetables couldn't stay under wraps forever. By the mid-1980s,

organic growers in California like Doug Gosling, then garden manager of the Farrallones Institute in Occidental, and Michael Maltus, manager of the garden at Fetzer Vineyard in Hopland, were growing tomatoes, eggplants, and peppers in a rainbow of colors. Meanwhile, the Seed Savers organization in Decorah, Iowa was collecting hundreds of colorful varieties including watermelons with yellow or orange flesh and purple tomatoes and sweet potatoes and reintroducing them to the public.

At about the same time, I visited the New York Botanical Garden and mentioned my color experiments to Debra Lerer, then director of children's gardening. Immediately inspired, Debra felt the desire to grow a rainbow garden in the children's section of the

Farmer's markets are a great place to seek out colorful vegetable varieties and find out which grow best in your climate. Craig and Toku Beccio *(above)*, owners of Happy Boy Farms of San Juan Bautista, California, offer many different colors of organically grown tomatoes, peppers, and potatoes.

botanical garden the next summer. Why hadn't I thought of that? Of course! Children and colorful vegetables were a natural combination and yet another reason to grow these vegetables. Visiting Debra later, I saw that the plot of rainbow vegetables was clearly a big hit. The children thought it much more fun to grow yellow zucchini than green. The purple potatoes were great because the young gardeners could show their parents vegetables they had never seen before. And the youngsters dubbed the purple beans "magic beans" because they turned green when cooked.

In the 1990s the movement toward colorful vegetables was well under way. Heirloom vegetables were going mainstream. Organic farmers, ever on the look out for an edge over the grocery store, found that colorful heirloom vegetables sold well. Seed company owners like Renee Shepherd of Renee's Garden and Rose Marie Nichols McGee of Nichols Garden Nursery offered many colorful varieties. And garden books and magazine articles routinely recommended them.

In recent years, yet another reason to grow rainbow vegetables has emerged. Nutritionists and plant breeders now know that vivid color often goes hand-in-hand with additional health benefits. Colorful varieties often yield more vitamins A and C and have more disease-fighting chemicals than some of their drab cousins. In the new millennium gardeners will find more and more vegetables like the red carrot and the orange tomato with extra beta carotene as many vegetable breeders select for these beneficial traits.

Saving a gene pool, making children's gardening more fun, and growing super nutritious vegetables are all excellent reasons to become a rainbow vegetable maven. And then there are the reasons that hooked me in the first place—growing rainbow vegetables is really great fun and harvesting a rainbow garden is an aesthetic experience in itself. Picture yourself taking a large basket into the garden to harvest your rainbow of vegetables and flowers. Place the red chard and pungent red nasturtiums into the basket. Move on to the golden beets and sunny calendulas. Your succulent yellow tomatoes and the yellow zucchini might be next. Add green, sweet, and ripe tomatoes and green radishes if you have some; these will make you chuckle. Dig up a few blue potatoes and finish the rainbow array with a luminescent 'Rosa Bianco' eggplant and purple string beans. No matter how many times I gather my vibrant rainbow vegetables, harvesting still makes me smile.

_____

'Bright Lights' chard _(below)_ comes in a mix of colors. Here, bright orange and yellow chard plants shine in a flower/vegetable border.

how to grow a rainbow garden

With a few exceptions, most unusually colored vegetables grow much like standard vegetables. For detailed information, consult "The Rainbow Vegetable Encyclopedia." For the nuts and bolts of soil preparation, fertilizing, watering, composting, mulching, and garden maintenance, see Appendix A.

Starting with Seeds

A small number of rainbow varieties are a little challenging to grow; for example, yellow beets are somewhat harder to germinate than the red varieties. Also, the all-red and the all-blue potato varieties usually yield half as much as most modern hybrids, so you must plant more than the regular amount.

Quite a few rainbow vegetables, however, are downright advantageous. For example, purple beans, blue-podded peas, and golden zucchinis are easier for gardeners to find on the vines than the usual varieties. As unpicked peas and beans make the vines less productive, with colorful vegetables you need not wonder why the beans and peas have stopped producing or what to do with a three-foot zucchini that has grown unnoticed for a week or two. 'Hopi Blue' corn needs less water than the average corn crop. And purple and yellow string bean varieties can be started in much cooler soil than standard string beans. Purple and orange cauliflower varieties need no garden blanching to be tender and sweet. The only real problem with growing a rainbow garden is locating the seeds of

Renee's Garden seeds sprays the seeds of their colorful vegetable mixes with dyes *(above)*. The color-coded seeds help gardeners know which color vegetable the plants will produce. Colorful herbs and vegetables *(right)* can sparkle in a mixed border. 'Red Rubin' basil has been planted among lemon basil and species orange zinnias at the Kendall Jackson Winery display gardens in Santa Rosa, California.

Growing more than one color of snap beans makes the harvest more appealing. Pictured above are three varieties of bush beans in one bed: yellow 'Roc d'Or,' 'Purple Queen,' and green 'Slenderette.' All are available in one package from Renee's Garden.

Rainbow flowers and vegetables make a Technicolor presentation. In the basket *(opposite)* are 'Burpee's Golden' beet, 'Gypsy' peppers, 'Ruby Red' chard, 'Mandarin Cross' tomato, 'Gold Rush' zucchini, and 'Albina Verduna' white beets.

some varieties. While the market is changing, many unique varieties are not readily available from local nurseries. The seed companies listed in the Resources section are good places to start.

Color Planning before Planting

The color range of your harvest will be a major planning consideration. You'll need to pay particular attention to the number of plants to grow, and to selecting and coordinating particular varieties. For example, the special effect of some colorful vegetables depends on lots of different colored varieties being served together. Envision three colors, not one, of tomatoes or peppers arranged on a tray. To achieve that effect, you'll want

to grow two plants of three or four varieties where possible instead of three or four plants of one or two varieties. For a mix of color with root vegetables and lettuces, forgo planting one row of each color. Instead, mix the seeds of many colors of beets, carrots, or radishes and sprinkle them together in the planting bed. In most cases you'll be able to tell the colors apart when you harvest because beets have distinct foliage and most shoulders of these vegetables show above the soil. (See the interview with Renee Shepherd for more information on mixing colorful vegetables in the same bed. Her seed company, Renee's Garden, offers packages of mixed colors of vegetables and the seeds are color-coded so you can see which colors you are planting.)

7

designing a rainbow garden

Cheryl Chang *(above)* helps to harvest the glorious bounty from the Hidden Villa rainbow garden. Meanwhile, the Hawthorne family, including Noah, Marcy, and baby Sierra *(opposite),* visit and enjoy the Hidden Villa garden under the watchful eye of "The Rainbow Lady" scarecrow.

When I first planted colorful vegetables, I primarily focused on their use in the kitchen. Finding many rainbow varieties more lovely in the garden than their monochromatic cousins, I soon started planning gardens that featured their bright colors. About the same time I became fascinated with colorful vegetables, I developed an interest in edible flowers. Again, their enticing colors drew me to them. Soon my passion for edible flowers and colorful vegetables dovetailed and I often grew them together. My favorite combinations became purple and pink violas and tulips with burgundy lettuces; orange and yellow nasturtiums and calendulas among the red and orange chards and beets; red onions and scallions with red dianthus; and 'Lemon Gem' marigolds interplanted with orange and yellow peppers.

With each garden I've grown, the rainbow effect gets stronger and the palette of plants expands. My first rainbow garden looked mostly green. Even though the radish roots were red and the corn kernels blue, their green foliage gave little hint of the unique vegetables. To enhance the impression of a rainbow garden, I've learned to include flowering plants in primary colors such as zinnias, salvias, violas, statice, calendulas, and marigolds. At first, I randomly interspersed the flowers. Now, for my favorite rainbow gardens, I arrange separate beds for the red, orange, yellow, green plants. Using poetic license, I combine the purple, indigo, and blue plants in the fifth bed.

Checking the Site

When planning a rainbow garden, I use the same techniques as when designing landscapes for my clients. My first step is to make sure the light exposure is correct. Most all edible plants need at least six hours of midday sun to survive; eight hours is better. I check for good rich soil and great drainage. (Appendix A includes information on soil preparation.) Then I compile a list of the vegetables to grow, noting each plant's height and spread, and which varieties grow best in my climate.

Drawing to Scale

My next step is to draw the garden area to scale, one-quarter inch equaling one foot. Graph paper or an architect's vellum with a grid for one-quarter-inch scale drawings is helpful. The vellum is available from drafting supply stores and can be purchased by the sheet. With my scale drawing and vegetable list ready, I design the garden.

I start by noting the garden's southernmost point on the scale drawing. This is important because I want the tallest plants situated on the garden's south side so they don't shade the shorter plants. I also plan paths or locate stepping stones for easy access to weed and harvest.

Creating the Rainbow

Next I plan the beds according to the order of the colors in the rainbow—red, orange, yellow, green, and a combination of the blue and purple tones. It's fun to select red vegetables for the

cutting flowers and vegetables and a few edible flowers, and my own winter Wizard of Oz garden filled with unusual colored vegetables and lots of edible flowers.

[note]

Make sure the flowers you are going to eat are edible and are not sprayed with commercial pesticides unfit for human consumption. The most versatile species in the kitchen and in a rainbow vegetable garden are: borage (blue), broccoli (yellow), calendulas (yellow and orange), chives (lavender), dianthus (red), species marigolds 'Lemon Gem' and 'Tangerine Gem' (yellow and orange), mustards (yellow), nasturtiums (orange, yellow, and red), dwarf runner beans 'Scarlet Bees' (red), tulips (orange, yellow, lavender, red), violas, pansies, and Johnny-jump-ups (lavender, blue, purple, yellow, and orange).

red beds, orange varieties for the orange beds, and so on. I flesh out the unusual colors with the more common varieties by adding, say, orange carrots to the orange bed and red beets to the red bed. Using the height and spread data from my plant list, I arrange the red row from back to front, choosing the tallest plants for the back, south side. For example, the twelve-foot-tall 'Bloody Butcher' corn would be in the back row, the six-foot-tall red tomatoes situated in front of the corn, and the two-and-one-half-foot-tall red peppers and maybe some red chard in front of the tomatoes. Then I plan the orange-, yellow-, green-, and blue-tone beds in the same manner, from back to front.

After selecting the vegetables, I choose ornamental or edible and ornamental flowers in bright primary colors to give an all-over rainbow effect. I intersperse bright, clear red flowers in the red rows, placing the tall varieties in the back and the shorter ones in the front. I place clear orange flowers in the orange row and so on.

Through the years I have designed many rainbow gardens including a preplanned rainbow garden kit for W. Atlee Burpee & Co. I never tire of the process and the fabulous gardens that result. The following pages include specific examples of a few of my rainbow gardens. They include a summer garden at Hidden Villa in Los Alto Hills, California, filled with colorful

The Hidden Villa Rainbow Garden

Hidden Villa is a magical place, an oasis of untamed nature in the midst of suburbia. It is the dream of Josephine and Frank Duveneck who envisioned preserving hundreds of wild acres for future generations to enjoy. Thousands of city children visit during the school year. In the summer, Hidden Villa becomes a children's camp filled with the smell of bay leaves underfoot, and the culinary delights from a very large vegetable garden.

A number of years ago—completely immersed in colorful veggies and knowing children loved them too—I was looking for a place to plant my fantasy of a huge rainbow vegetable garden. As I live not far from Hidden Villa, it seemed a perfect place for my culinary rainbow.

Once the Hidden Villa trustees gave approval, I turned to the local junior college horticulture department for help with this ambitious project. The professor recommended Gudi Riter, which led to a fortuitous pairing as Gudi is a talented cook as well as gardener. You will enjoy trying many of the recipes she helped me develop.

Because Gudi and I were planting so many unusual colors of vegetables, and to some extent flowers, we planned our garden early in the year (January) to have a good selection of colorful varieties. We needed plenty of time to order seeds and get the peppers, eggplants, and tomatoes sown in late February. In late March, we started more flats of flowers and vegetables including chard, scallions, parsley, and basil, and the

flowering zinnias, statice, salvia, verbena, safflower, species marigolds, kochia, and 'Bells of Ireland.' Before we planted in late April, the folks at Hidden Villa plowed the area, which was about twenty feet deep and a hundred feet long, and divided the plot into five twenty-foot-square sections approximately five rows deep. They also mixed in lots of manure.

Gudi finished the soil preparation by laying out and digging the beds and paths. With the help of her son and daughter, soon we were able to plant much of the garden. We placed our transplants then seeded the beans, corn, amaranth, beets, carrots, potatoes, and sunflowers in place. The area was so very large; we'd underestimated the number of plants to fill the rows. So we purchased dwarf marigolds, lobelia, and verbena transplants from a nursery.

The garden got off to a great start with the exception of most of the blue potatoes that rotted. A few gophers gave us problems until they were trapped. By late June the garden was filling in very well.

By then, the area's grasses and brush had dried up. In California, we get no rain from May through September. Consequently, the deer moved out of the woods and down the hillside into our rainbow garden. In a flurry of creativity we decided to outline the different beds with a kaleidoscope of yarns. Besides initially foiling the deer, the bright strands gave more of a rainbow feeling to the garden. When the camp children arrived, the garden had yet to bloom but the colorful yarn outlines gave a hint of the fun

to follow. Although the yarn seemed to confuse the deer for a few weeks, soon they were back.

We then tried a scarecrow—a lady built from stockings and straw and dressed in one of my dresses straight from the 1970s, my quasi-hippie stage. This only kept the deer at bay for a few more weeks.

We finally resorted to black plastic bird netting placed here and there and resigned ourselves to some damage.

Despite the hungry intruders, by the end of July we started harvesting lots of vegetables and flowers. The camp cooks used some; we fed our families; and we even started bringing neighbors and friends to help. Let me tell you, two thousand square feet of vegetables is a lot of vegetables. We all seemed most to enjoy assembling large harvests of vegetables and flowers and arranging them by colors to really experience the rainbow effect.

The Hidden Villa rainbow garden came to a close in October and we deemed it a great success. It introduced hundreds of visiting schoolchildren to unusual colors and varieties of vegetables. The garden looked really "cool" and attracted the local TV station to come do a story. Most of all, we shared an exciting summer full of surprises in our special place. I'm sure the Duvenecks are smiling.

Clockwise from top left: Gudi Riter, her son Andy, and daughter Tina plan out the marigolds for the orange row in the Hidden Villa rainbow garden; Sandra Chang sorts her rainbow treasures in the Hidden Villa garden; Gudi sorts the vegetables from the Hidden Villa garden by color.

Red Row

4- to 6-foot plants for back row
'Burgundy' amaranth, grain type
'Illumination' amaranth, leaf type
'Bloody Butcher' corn
'Red' okra
'Red Currant' tomato

2- to 3-foot plants
'Big Red' zinnia
Hibiscus sabdariffa— annual
  hibiscus
'Early Red' bell pepper
'Serrano' chile pepper
'Anaheim' chile pepper
'Ruby' chard

1- to 2-foot plants
'Detroit Dark Red' beets
'Flare' salvia
'Red Beard' scallions

Plants under one foot
'Peter Pan' scarlet dwarf zinnia
'Romance' red verbena

Orange Row

4- to 6-foot plants for back row
'Large Flowered Mix' ornamental
  sunflowers
Orange tithonia
'Golden Jubilee' tomato
'Mandarin Cross' tomato

2- to 3-foot plants
'X-20' marigold
Safflower
Apricot statice

1- to 2-foot plants
'Golden Belle' pepper
'Tequila Sunrise' chile pepper
'Habañero' peppers

Plants under one foot
'Orange Gem' marigolds
'Gold Nugget' marigolds

Yellow Ro

**4- to 6-foot plants
  for back rows**
'Giganteus' sunflowe
'Teddy Bear' sunflow
'Taxi' tomato
'Yellow Pear' tomato
'Yellow Currant' toma
'X-15' marigold

2- to 3-foot plants
'Sunburst' summer
  squash
'Gold Rush' zucchini

1- to 2-foot plants
'Pencil Pod Wax' sna
  beans
'Gypsy' bell pepper
'Burpee's Golden' be

Plants under one fo
'Lemon Gem' marigo
'Yellow Sophia' mari
Golden sage

Green Row

4- to 6-foot plants
'Italian White' sunflowers
'Bells of Ireland'

2- to 3-foot plants
Kochia
'Envy' green zinnia
'Burpee Hybrid' zucchini
'California Wonder' bell pepper
'Jalapeno' chile pepper

1- to 2-foot plants
'Burpee's Tender Pod' bush snap
   beans

Plants under one foot
'Spicy Globe' dwarf basil
French thyme
'Extra-curled Dwarf' parsley
Chamomile

Purple Row

4- to 6-feet plants
'Hopi Blue' corn
'Purple Striped-leaf' ornamental
   corn
'Sicilian Purple' artichoke

2- to 3-foot plants
Purple zinnia
Deep blue statice
'Royalty Purple Pod' bush snap
   beans
'Rosa Bianco' eggplant
'Dusky' eggplant

1- to 2-foot plants
'Victoria' blue salvia
'Opal' purple basil

Plants under one foot
'Buddy' dwarf purple gomphrena
'Crystal Palace' blue lobelia
'Blue Mink' ageratum

The Rainbow
Oz Garden

Many, many years ago I removed the front lawn and planted a vegetable garden in my sunny front yard. I had become weary of trying to grow sun-loving plants in a shady area. As a landscape designer I knew I could make my garden lovely enough for a formal suburban neighborhood; judging from everyone's reaction I succeeded. A fallout from front yard gardening I had not anticipated was that neighborhood children would come to visit and want to be involved. After a few years we were having lots of fun together and I found myself moving away from formal vegetable gardens and leaning more toward what "my kids" wanted. One year, that meant lots of flowers for drying; another summer we planted huge pumpkins. From one year to another I found myself growing more of their favorite rainbow-colored vegetables. Eventually I decided that while I had already grown a rainbow garden at Hidden Villa, it had been a summer garden. This time I would fill my rainbow garden with cool-season vegetables and grow them during the winter. Thanks to "my kids," my garden style really loosened up. I thought, "Why not plan the garden with a Wizard of Oz theme and design it around a yellow brick road?" Well, that idea met with enthusiastic hoorays. All the kids on the street from ages three to ninety deemed it a spectacular idea.

I designed a graceful, curving path through my front garden; my crew installed a brick path and painted it a bright, bright yellow. Getting in the spirit of the project my daughter-in-law Julie Creasy and assistant Gudi Riter started sewing costumes. Dorothy and the Scarecrow were stuffed with straw and dressed delightfully. My friend and the artist who drew the line drawings in this book, Marcy Hawthorne, painted Dorothy's face. Barbara Burkhart assembled the Tin Man from five-gallon nursery containers, hand trowels, a hose nozzle, and a plastic watering can; she sprayed him with chrome paint.

By the time the brick path was complete it was really too late to put in a cool-season garden. Instead, for a summer garden we planted the Oz garden with corn and lots of zinnias. It sure was a lot of fun but by early September we were ready for the main event—"The Rainbow Oz Garden". Out came the corn and zinnias and in went the cool-season vegetables. I designed color-matched beds on both sides of the yellow brick road and placed the shortest plants next to the road and the tallest the furthest away. Unlike the plot at Hidden Villa, no plants were very tall so planting them at the garden's northern end was not an issue. I chose edible flowers of clear, bright, solid colors to fill in the beds; they also gave the garden and my salads a festive look.

Both the summer and winter Oz gardens became a neighborhood institution—a part of Sunday family strolls. More than once I saw some of the kids skip down the path on their way to school. Delivery people said it was the favorite address on their route; joggers and walkers told me they found them-

selves drawn to the street. The most fun, though, was picking baskets of those colorful vegetables and flowers and laying them out in their glory for all of us to admire.

The scarecrow sits between the yellow and orange rows of the Creasy Oz rainbow vegetable garden. His harvest includes the many colors of 'Bright Lights' Swiss chard, 'Burpee's Golden' beets, 'Detroit Dark Red' beets, 'Stockton' red onions, garlic, 'Easter Egg' radishes, and 'Danver's Half Long' carrots. Behind him a broccoli plant flowers, attracting beneficial insects to keep the pests under control.

Plant List:

~

The Oz Rainbow Garden

Red Rows

2- to 3-foot plants
'Ruby' chard
'Detroit Dark Red' beets
'Stockton Red' onions
'General Eisenhower' red tulips

Plants under one foot
'Juliet' red lettuce
'Telstar Crimson' dianthus
'Red Empress' nasturtiums

Orange Rows

2- to 3-foot plants
'Bright Lights' orange chard
'Danvers Half Long' orange
   carrots
'Royal Chantenay' orange carrots
'Orange Sun' orange tulips
'Pacific Beauty' orange
   calendulas

Plants under one foot
'Orange Crystal Bowl' violas

Yellow Rows

2- to 3-foot plants
'Bright Lights' yellow chard
'Burpee's Golden' beets
'Pacific Giant' yellow calendulas
'Garant' yellow tulips
'Yellow Sweet Spanish' onions

Plants under one foot
Golden sage
Golden lemon thyme
'Yellow Crystal Bowl' violas

Green Rows

2- to 3-foot plants
'Premium Crop' broccoli
'De Cicco' broccoli
'Romy' fennel

Plants under one foot
'Nevada' crisp-head lettuce
'Nordic II' spinach
'Tres Fine Maraichere' endive
'Triple Curled' parsley

Purple/Blue Rows

2- to 3-foot plants
'Osaka Purple' Japanese mustard
'All Blue' potatoes
'Tokyo Mix' ornamental cabbages
'Attila' purple tulips
'Purplette' scallions

Plants under one foot
'Easter Egg' radishes
Johnny-jump-ups
'Blue Princess' violas
'King Henry' purple violas

Renee Shepherd

Renee Shepherd and I have been friends and colleagues for years. Both of us are fascinated with colorful vegetables. Researching this book gave me the excuse to ask her to share her views. "Before I even get them in the kitchen I enjoy these vivid vegetables," Renee began. "Picking a basket filled with many colors is beautiful. Food in vibrant colors is more exciting. I enjoy simple cooking. And simple dishes made with diverse colors seem more complex. For example, if I cook up green snap beans and sprinkle them with crumbled feta cheese, it's interesting. However, if I cook both yellow and green snap beans together, the recipe becomes exciting."

"Then there is the satisfaction of growing all these special exotics from seeds," Renee continued. "Growing three varieties of a vegetable instead of one extends my interest in the crop. It's like taking a theme and adding a variation. I find it hard to imagine why someone wouldn't want to grow vegetables in many colors."

Renee is the owner of a new seed company, Renee's Garden. Her seed packets are perfect for the rainbow gardener. For instance, she offers a trio of cayenne peppers in one package: a purple variety, a red pepper, and a yellow one. The beets come in three colors as do the tomatoes, zucchini, snap beans, bell peppers, lettuces, etc. So the gardener doesn't need to buy three different seed packages of the same vegetable to get the rainbow effect. Further, the gardener needn't research whether the vegetables will ripen at the same time. Renee has done all the work for you.

"I was flying cross-country when the idea

came to me," Renee explained. "Then I puzzled over how to color-code the seeds so gardeners could tell which color they were growing. No rainbow gardener wants to start seeds from a multi-color package and end up with four red bell pepper seedlings, one yellow variety, and no orange. There had to be a way to mark the seeds. Easter egg dyes came to mind because they are nontoxic and readily available. As soon as I got home, I tried spritzing the seeds with different colors. Sure enough, the dye dried quickly and left just enough stain so you could tell the different colors apart."

Renee Shepherd, seeds woman extraordinaire, has long been enamored with colorful vegetables. Her latest seed company, Renee's Garden, offers a rainbow in a package. For instance, she sells red, yellow, and orange bell pepper seeds all in one package. The gardener can tell the colors of the pepper varieties apart because Renee has dyed the seeds.

Renee's colorful menus are famous. I remember the time she roasted bell peppers of many colors and drizzled them with olive oil, balsamic vinegar, and melted anchovies (see recipe, page 76). Then there's her exotic salad made with multicolored 'Easter Egg' radishes combined with the sweetness of fennel and apples (see recipe, page 70). Renee adapted her Aunt Alice's braised summer squash recipe with dill. Rather than using only one color of summer squash like her aunt, Renee combines yellow, dark-green, and light-green summer squash and carrots in the chicken broth (see recipe, page 78). She also likes to make a confetti of dry red and yellow cayenne flakes to sprinkle over pizza. Asked how she serves tomatoes of many colors, Renee said, "I love the different colored cherry tomatoes—I call them garden candy. They're so sweet and jewel-like. I stir fry them lightly until they start to burst, then add herbs and garlic and serve them as a warm salad. Sometimes I arrange large colorful tomatoes slices over a tart or I hollow out tomatoes and stuff them with an orzo pasta stuffing. Another of my favorite ways to feature their colors is to make two sauces, one of red and the other of orange tomatoes, and create a pool of color and flavor on the plate for roasted vegetables."

Renee has done a great deal to expand the home gardeners' seed choices by offering her seeds in many retail nurseries and homestores. Rainbow gardeners no longer have to mail away for colorful varieties. I, for one, am very grateful.

the rainbow vegetable encyclopedia

The vegetable varieties I have chosen for this encyclopedia are those that are the most colorful, whether it be in the garden, in the kitchen, or both.

For me, vegetable gardens are beautiful and the addition of especially colorful varieties often makes them even more lovely. Further, given their beauty, many of these plants are suitable for edible landscapes—in a flower border say, or in containers on the patio.

Growing colorful vegetables is a rather new phenomenon, and unlike their more common relatives, some "rainbow" vegetable varieties are hard to obtain, available only from one or two seed sources, say. I have noted sources for many of the unusual varieties.

In the average kitchen there are already many colorful vegetable vari-

'Fire Dance' cabbage *(opposite)* is one of many varieties of red cabbage that can brighten a garden corner.

eties—red beets and orange carrots come to mind. In this encyclopedia, however, I have ignored the familiar ones, my emphasis instead is with vegetables that by today's standards are considered eccentric or to be unusually colored. (As an aside, food color biases change from culture to culture and with the times, so for example, 200 years ago in Europe instead of red tomatoes and beets, people preferred yellow varieties and instead of white cauliflower they favored purple.)

The colors in vegetables are the result of different pigments. The presence of particular carotenoids, for instance, will cause a carrot to be orange and certain anthocyanins are responsible for a cabbage being red. Some of these pigments are stable, others are destroyed by heat or are water soluble, and in the latter cases the vivid color disappears. Further, some vegetables turn brown when cut and exposed to the air. As the emphasis in this book is to feature vivid colors on the table, where possible, I have included this type of information.

The color of a vegetable often correlates to its nutrition content and I have included some of this information as well. For an overview of how pigments and the color of vegetables respond to cooking, see the section on "Cooking with Colors" on page 64, and for more information on the nutrients in vegetables, see page 62.

For the basic information on soil preparation, mulching, composting, irrigation, and organic controls for pests and diseases see Appendices A and B on pages 90 and 96.

'Illumination' amaranth

AMARANTH

Amaranthus hypochondriacus,
A. cruentus, A gangeticus,
A. tricolor

AMARANTH IS BEAUTIFUL IN THE garden and nutritious in the kitchen. The leaves and seed heads can be red, purple, green, cream, or a combination. Use the tall varieties in the back of vegetable and flower beds and the shorter ones in the middle of the border.

How to grow: Amaranth glories in warm weather. Start seedlings after any danger of frost has passed. Plant seeds $1/8$ inch deep, 4 inches apart, in full sun, in rich, well-drained soil. Plant the large-grain amaranths in blocks with the rows 1 foot apart to prevent lodging. Thin the plants to 1 foot apart and keep the plants fairly moist. Generally, amaranth grows with great enthusiasm. The leaf-types grow to 2 feet, some of the grain varieties to 6 feet. Cucumber beetles are occasionally a problem.

Harvest the leaf-types when they are young. Harvest the grains after the first frost in the North; in mild-winter areas wait until seeds begin to drop. Lay harvested tops on a tarp in the sun to dry for about a week; protect against rain and heavy dew. Thresh the grains by laying the heads on sheets—then step on them, to knock the seeds free (or rub the seed heads with on a screen; wear gloves to prevent your hands from being stained when processing the red varieties). Use an electric fan to separate the seeds from the lighter chaff as you pour them into a container.

Varieties

The leaves and seeds of all varieties can be eaten, but the leaf-types have the tastiest leaves and the grain-types have more seeds.

Grain Amaranths

'All Red': 5 feet tall; extremely deep red leaves with red plumes; does not readily fall over

'Golden Giant': 110 days; 6 feet tall with beautiful golden stems and flower heads; grown for its white grain and edible young leaves; high yielding

'Hopi Red Dye' ('Komo'): 120 days; to 6 feet tall; reddish-purple

'Purple Amaranth': 110 days; 6 feet tall; green-red variegated foliage; reddish-purple and green seed heads

Leaf Amaranths

'Illumination': spectacular magenta, pink, to crimson leaves born upper third of plant, grows to 5 feet; often used as a garnish

'Joseph's Coat' (tricolor): 70 days; a spectacular tricolor variety from India with red, cream, and green leaves

'Merah': 75–80 days; leaf-type with crinkled green and red leaves

How to prepare: In theory, because the red pigments in amaranths are betacyanin like red beets, the color should be stable when cooked, but I find the red amaranth leaves I've cooked often turn pale and grayish. Obviously there is more to learn about amaranth colors. To enjoy red amaranth leaves I select young, tender leaves from the leaf-types and use them raw in salads or as a spectacular garnish. I cook the green varieties as I would spinach. The leaves are very nutritious and high in calcium and iron.

Amaranth grain has a mild and nutty flavor, is high in protein, and contains essential amino acids. It can be cooked and eaten alone or mixed with other ingredients. It contains no gluten so must be combined with wheat flour to make risen breads. The seed can be popped like popcorn; stir $1/2$ cup of seeds in a hot frying pan for about 30 seconds or until popped. Mix with honey to create a traditional confection from Mexico.

ARTICHOKES, PURPLE
Cynara scolymus

THE ARTICHOKE IS A GIANT thistle whose flower buds, when cooked, are deliciously edible. The plant is fountain shaped and grows to about 4 feet tall and almost as wide. The flower buds are usually green, but some varieties have purple buds.

How to grow: Artichokes prefer cool, moist summers and mild winters but tolerate summer heat if the soil is kept moist. Give them full sun in mild areas and partial shade in hot-summer climates. Below 28°F they need winter protection, for example an overturned basket filled with leaves placed above the roots. In coldest-winter areas bring the roots inside during winter and keep them moist and cool. In hot, early summers the artichoke buds open too soon and are tough.

Green varieties of artichokes are started when bare root from plants are

'Violetto' artichokes

'Violetto' artichoke buds

offered in spring. (Bare-root plants are dug up while dormant and sold with their roots wrapped in plastic.) In contrast, the purple variety of artichoke is usually started from seeds. In cold climates, sow seeds indoors eight weeks before your last spring frost date, about ¼ inch deep and ¼ inch apart. In mild climates, fall plantings work well too. When sowing, soil temperature should be between 70°F to 80°F. Transplant seedlings to 4-inch pots. Grow at cooler temperatures (70°F during the day, 60°F at night). Transplant to the garden when 8 weeks old. (Spring plantings need at least 250 hours of temperatures under 50°F to induce budding.) Protect from frost.

Artichokes require rich, moist, well-drained soil with plenty of organic matter. They respond well to deep mulches and manure. Extra nitrogen should be added halfway through the growing season and after harvest. Dig up and thin plants every three years.

Aphids, earwigs, and snails are sometimes a problem.

When harvesting, cut off young artichoke buds, about 4 inches below the bud, well before they start to open. The younger the bud, the more tender it is and the more of it that is edible.

Varieties

The Cook's Garden, Redwood City Seed Company, and The Gourmet Gardener carry seeds of purple artichokes.

'Purple Sicilian': produces bronzy-purple buds

'Violetto': Italian variety; produces medium-sized, purple buds

How to prepare: The anthocyanins in purple artichokes lose their color when cooked, so serve them raw to emphasize the color. Raw artichokes once cut and thus exposed to the air, quickly turn brown. So to use them raw, keep them in water with added lemon juice to prevent discoloring.

How to prepare: In French kitchens, immature purple artichokes are traditionally served raw: the slightly bitter bud is cut into quarters, the stem end is dipped in salt, and the dish is accompanied by bread and sweet butter. In Italy, pieces of young, tender raw artichokes are dipped in olive oil as part of an antipasto, or the heart is thinly sliced and served drizzled with lemon juice, olive oil, and salt.

Young fresh buds can be eaten without removing the choke (fuzzy, inedible center). Most mature artichokes must have the choke removed, but homegrown ones, if harvested while still young, do not.

To prepare a mature artichoke bud, cut off the top inch or so of the leaves. Then, with your hand, peel back the outside layer of leaves to where they break readily. If there is a fuzzy choke at the bottom, scrape it out with a sharp spoon. Immediately soak them in acidulated water until you are ready to cook them.

Whole artichokes can be stuffed and baked, steamed, or boiled in water with the juice of two lemons. Cook them until a knife inserted in the bottom of the choke is tender and present them whole. To eat a whole artichoke, pull off the outside leaves and use your teeth to scrape out the flesh. The remaining heart, or bottom, is cut into bite-size pieces and relished.

Artichokes may also be incorporated into many cooked dishes. Trim tender small bulbs lightly and use whole or use the hearts of larger bulbs cut in pieces in salads or casseroles.

ASPARAGUS, PURPLE
Asparagus officinalis

ASPARAGUS IS AN HERBACEOUS perennial that goes dormant in winter; its edible spears appear in spring. Asparagus shoots, whether they are green or purple, not cut for eating develop into airy, ferny foliage plants 5 feet high that can line a walkway or serve as a billowy background in a flower bed.

How to grow: Asparagus grows in all but the most hot and cold climates. The green varieties, and one purple variety are available as one-year-old rooted crows (the base of the plant plus roots). A family of four will need thirty to forty plants. Because asparagus plants remain in one place for many years and are heavy feeders, the soil must be prepared very well. Asparagus needs a deep organic soil, with a pH of 6.5. Excellent drainage is critical. Asparagus plants also need full sun.

In the early spring, prepare the soil and remove any perennial weeds. For thirty to forty plants, spade up the area as follows: dig two trenches 6 inches deep (a foot in coldest areas), 12 inches wide, about 20 feet long, and 3 feet apart. Amend the soil in the trenches with compost or aged manure and 4 pounds of bone meal worked 8 inches into the soil. Then place the crowns in the bottom, 15 inches apart with their roots well spread out. Cover with 2 inches of soil. As the shoots emerge,

continue to fill the trench with soil. Once the trenches are full, mulch with 4 inches of an organic mulch.

On normal soil, annual applications of compost or modest amounts of chicken manure is all that is needed for fertilizer. After the first season, only moderate amounts of water are needed during the growing season. In the arid Southwest, to encourage dormancy do not irrigate in winter.

Asparagus beetles are generally the most serious pest. Diligent hand picking of the beetles in early spring as soon as they appear helps reduce the population. If the beetles are taking over, knock them off into a bucket of soapy water or use a Bt (*Bacillus thuringiensis*) developed for their control and apply it according to directions. Further, fall cleanup removes some of the breeding adults. If the bed is free of beetles from planting time on, use floating row covers to keep them out.

A fungus disease called asparagus rust can be a problem in damp weather. Cercospora leaf spot can be a serious problem in the Southeast. Where gophers are numerous they can destroy the whole bed. Plant the crowns in wire baskets to protect them. Perennial weeds can quickly take over and crowd out a bed of asparagus, so remove all weeds and keep the bed mulched.

Harvest the spears by snapping them off an inch above soil level. No harvest is recommended the first year. In the second year, limit the harvest to three weeks. In subsequent years, harvest for six to eight weeks, and until the spears begin to thin to a pencil thickness.

'Purple Sweet' asparagus

Fertilize with fish meal after the harvest. In mild climates, cut down plants when they turn brown; in cold climates wait until early spring as the stalks help maintain a snow cover.

Varieties
'Purple Sweet' ('Sweet Purple'): old variety; large, tender, deep burgundy spears; sweet flavor; Park Seed Company and R. H. Shumway's carry this variety as rooted crowns

How to prepare: The purple pigments in asparagus are anthocyanins and they fade quickly when cooked. Young shoots are delicious raw in salads or served with flavorful dips. If you cook the purple asparagus, simmer it in an inch of water with $1/4$ cup of lemon juice to help maintain some of the color, the longer you cook it the more color it loses, so whenever possible serve them al dente.

BASIL

Ocimum basilicum

WHILE THERE ARE MANY TYPES of basil, the ones we are interested here have purple foliage.

How to grow: Basils are annual herbs that glory in hot weather and wither with frost. Plant it in full sun in fertile, well-drained soil with much organic matter. Start basil seeds inside a month before the weather warms up in spring, or use transplants from the nursery. Place plants about 1 foot apart and keep them moist during the grow-ing season. Fertilize with a balanced organic fertilizer every six weeks and after a large harvest.

Occasional pests are slugs and snails, and cucumber and Japanese beetles. When harvesting, leaves are picked by hand or cut. Keep the flower-heads continually cut back or the plant will go to seed and give few leaves.

Varieties

'Osmin Purple': purple leaves and stems; glossy, slightly ruffled leaves; fragrant; lavender flowers

'Red Rubin': purple leaves; fragrant; pink flowers; similar to the old standby 'Dark Opal' but more uniform

'Purple Ruffles': dark purple, ruffled leaves; fragrant; lavender flowers; seedlings are variable, select most colorful plants as you thin

How to prepare: The purple basils are high in anthocyanins. To best enjoy the color, use these basils raw in salads, sandwiches, and as a garnish. They will lend some of their pink color to vinegars and apple jelly. If you cook, puree, or mince purple basils though, they turn a disappointing brown.

'Red Rubin' basil and Lemon Basil

'Royalty Purple Pod'

'Dragon's Tongue'

'Wax Romano'

BEANS
PURPLE AND YELLOW SNAP BEANS
Phaseolus vulgaris

PURPLE AND YELLOW SNAP BEANS are more popular with children than their green cousins.

How to grow: Beans are adaptable annuals and are planted after all danger of frost is past. Purple and wax varieties can tolerate colder soil than most green snap beans. They need full sun and a good, loose garden loam with plenty of added humus. Sow seeds of bush beans 1 inch deep in rows 18 inches apart; thin to 6 inches. Pole beans need a strong trellis to climb on. Plant the seeds 1 inch deep; thin to 8 inches apart. If the plants look pale midseason fertilize with fish emulsion. Beans are best watered deeply and infrequently.

Beans have their share of pests, including bean beetles, beanloopers, whiteflies, aphids, mites, and cucumber beetles. Anthracnose and leaf spots diseases are most prevalent in humid climates.

Harvest snap beans when the seeds inside are still very small and the pods are tender. Make sure to keep all beans harvested or the plants stop producing.

Varieties
Renee's Garden offers a combination package of green, purple, and yellow beans in retail stores.

Purple Snap Beans
'Hopi Purple String Beans': purple bean with black crescent-moon-shaped stripes; can be grown with little or no irrigation; available from Native Seeds/SEARCH

'Purple Queen': 55 days; bush; purple pods and flowers; sweet flavor; common bean mosaic-virus tolerant

'Royal Burgundy': 51 days; bush; dark purple pods; vigorous

'Royalty Purple Pod' ('Royalty'): bush; deep-purple pods and flowers; vigorous; some resistance to Mexican bean beetles

'Trionfo' ('Trionfo Violetto'): 65 days; pole; deep purple pods and lavender flowers; vigorous

Yellow Snap Beans
'Cherokee': 55 days; bush; sweet, wax bean; early; high yielding; widely adapted; rust and common bean mosaic-virus resistant

'Dragon's Tongue' ('Dragon Langerie'): 65 days; bush; unusual creamy yellow wax bean with pur-

'Pencil Pod Wax'

Renee's rainbow collection beans: green slenderette, 'Roc D'or,' and 'Purple Queen'

ple stripes; available from Bountiful
Gardens

'Pencil Pod Black Wax ('Pencil Pod'):
53 days; bush; tender yellow pods
with black seeds; early

'Roc D'or': 57 days; bush; slender yellow pods; productive; resistant to
common bean mosaic virus and
anthracnose

'Wax Romano': 58 days; bush; light
yellow pods with meaty texture;
vigorous

Yellow Anellino ('Gancetto Burro'):
80 days; pole; small, crescent-shaped
pods; rich bean flavor

How to prepare: Yellow wax beans
keep their color when cooked and are
used as you would any snap bean,
boiled or steamed until just tender,
though cooking times are short as the
beans turn to mush quickly. Try them
in a three-bean salad garnished with
raw purple beans. The purple beans
get their color from anthocyanins and
loose the purple color and turn a vivid
green when boiled for two minutes—
like magic—kids love to watch. (No
guess work to know if your purple
beans are properly blanched for freez-
ing, when the color changes from purple to green they are perfect.) Even
marinating them in vinegar or lemon
juice will eventually turn them green.
In my experience, making them into a
pureed soup creates a decidedly unappetizing gray soup.

To preserve the deep purple color,
serve the young beans raw in salads or
on a festive dip platter mixed with
other colorful vegetables.

Three colors of beets from Renee's Garden

BEETS
Beta vulgaris

THE ANCIENT GREEKS AND Romans appreciated both red and white beets; and yellow beets were popular in Europe for centuries.

How to grow: Sow beet seeds directly in rich, well-drained soil, in early spring or fall, in full sun. They can take some frost. Plant the seeds 1/4 inch deep in wide rows or broadcast over a 3-foot-wide bed. I like to mix colors of beet varieties in the same bed so I can combine them in a recipe. Plant extra seeds of the golden beets as they germinate poorly. Beet seeds are actually a cluster of seeds; therefore,

they must be thinned to 3 inches apart for full size beets—2 inches for babies. Fertilize midseason with a balanced organic fertilizer and water evenly.

Occasionally, leaf miners tunnel through the leaves. A fungus disease cercospora flourishes in humid conditions and makes orange spots on the foliage. A rust fungus can also be a problem.

Harvest when the beets are 3 inches across or less.

Varieties

Renee's Garden carries three colors of beets in the same package.

'Albina Verduna' ('Snow White'): 65 days; pure white; large and sweet

'Bull's Blood': 60 days, a beet grown

for its deep red leaves as well as the roots; some resistance to leaf miner; the "greens" retain most of their color when cooked; available from Garden City Seeds

'Chioggia': 50 days; red on outside, red and white peppermint-striped rings inside; sweet

'Burpee's Golden': 60 days; delicious, sweet yellow beets; leaf midribs are golden; low germination rates

How to prepare: The red pigments in beets are betacyanins; the yellow, betaxanthins. These pigments are fairly stable, though they do fade and change if food is overcooked. (If I boil my borscht too long it turns from a rich red to a dull reddish-brown.) Use

CABBAGES AND THEIR KIN

BROCCOLI
Brassica oleracea var. italica and B. oleracea. var. botrytis

BRUSSELS SPROUTS
B. oleracea var. gemmifera

CABBAGE
B. oleracea var. capitata and B. oleracea var. bulata

CAULIFLOWER
B. oleracea var. botrytis

KALE
B. oleracea var. acephala

KOHLRABI
B. oleracea var. gongylodes

MOST OF THIS FAMILY OF vegetables has green leaves and buds, but it is the purple or pink varieties we are most interested in here.

'Chioggia,' 'Burpee's Golden,' and 'Cylindra' *(above left)*; 'Albino Verduna' and 'Detroit Dark Red' *(above right)*; Doug Gosling and beet harvest *(below)*

beets raw or cooked in salads, cooked in soups and stews, or simply boiled or steamed and served with butter. The yellow, white, and the striped 'Chioggia' beets will not bleed and discolor the other ingredients in a cooked dish as do the red varieties and are great roasted in the oven with a little olive oil and garlic. To highlight yellow beets, serve them julienned with red ones or as baby beets. Note: pureed yellow beets sometimes oxidize, turning yellow-brown.

'Bull's Blood' greens are deep red and are one of the few "red" greens to retain their color and are a meltingly rich vegetable if steamed briefly. When the leaves are very young they are beautiful when added raw to a mixed salad.

How to grow: These vegetables are grown as cool-season annuals. They can bolt and become bitter-tasting in extremely hot weather. All need full sun, or light shade in hot climates.

Start most seeds indoors eight weeks before your last average frost date. Transplant them into rich soil filled with organic matter about two weeks before the last average frost date. (Start cauliflower a little earlier,

as it grows more slowly; start Brussels sprouts four weeks before the last frost date and transplant them in a month.) Most can also be planted in midsummer for a fall crop. Sow cabbage, broccoli, Brussels sprouts, and cauliflower seeds 3 inches apart, $1/2$ inch deep; thin or transplant small cabbages 12 inches apart and the larger cabbages, broccoli, Brussels sprouts, and cauliflower 24 inches apart. As they all tend to be top-heavy, when transplanting, place them lower in the soil than you would most vegetables—up to their first set of true leaves (the first leaves after the seed leaves). Plant kale seeds $1/2$ inch deep, 1 inch apart, and thin to about 1 foot. Unlike most cole crops, kohlrabi is best seeded in place, rather than started indoors. In early spring or late sum-

mer, sow kohlrabi seeds $1/4$ inch deep, 1 inch apart, thin to 4 inches for baby kohlrabi and 6 inches for full size. Work compost and one cup of a balanced organic fertilizer into the soil around each plant at planting time. A month after planting, side dress an organic nitrogen fertilizer scratched into the soil around the plants. Mulching helps retain moisture.

Most cabbage-family plants are susceptible to the same pests and diseases. (Kale tends to have far fewer problems than most.) Flea beetles, imported cabbageworm, cabbage root fly, and cutworms are potential problems. Use floating row covers to prevent these pests. You can also prevent the cabbage root fly from laying her eggs by placing black plastic directly over the roots

Chinese elogated cabbage, green drumhead, and red 'Ruby Perfection' cabbages *(above)*; 'Red Peacock' kale among lettuces *(below)*.

Purple sprouting broccoli *(above)*;
'Romanesco' broccoli *(below)*

'Red Russian' kale *(above)*; 'Lacinato'
kale *(below)*

open; once the primary head is harvested, smaller heads may form. Cauliflower heads are traditionally protected from the sun to keep the curds white and tender. In contrast, the orange and purple varieties we are interested in need direct sunlight to develop their colors. Harvest cauliflower heads at the base when they are full but before the curds begin to separate. Harvest a few very young kale leaves as they are needed and use them raw for salads. Use the more mature kale leaves for cooked dishes. Many varieties of kale winter over in most climates. Start harvesting kohlrabi bulbs once they are an inch across. The young small bulbs are best for eating raw.

Harvest Brussels sprouts in the fall or winter. Cold weather causes the purple color to be more vibrant and the flavors to mature. If the plants are kept well mulched with straw, sprouts often develop and mature well into the winter. Brussels sprouts mature up the stem, from the bottom to the top, so harvest in that direction when they are no larger than one inch in diameter.

Varieties

Broccoli

'Purple Spouting' ('Early Purple Sprouting'): 120 days; purple-green leaves and purple flower buds; to 3 feet high; very hardy

'Romanesco': 85 days; heads are an attractive, chartreuse, conical whorl of mild, sweet florets; large plant; extremely variable in form

'Violet Queen': 60 days: purple buds; early; uniform

Brussels Sprouts

'Rubine' ('Rubine Red'): clusters of red sprouts; red foliage; large; late; hardy; popular in Europe, carried by Bountiful Gardens

Cauliflower

Purple and orange cauliflowers are easier to grow than white varieties as

of the plant. Rotate members of the cabbage family with other vegetable families to prevent diseases.

Harvest cabbages anytime after they have started to form a ball, but before they split. If a hard freeze is expected, harvest all cabbages and store them in a cool place. Harvest broccoli when the buds begin to swell but before they

'White Peacock' kale *(above);* 'Miniature Flowering' cabbage and 'White Peacock' kale *(below)*

they do not require garden blanching (covering the leaves to prevent the sun from reaching them and making them tough).

'Orange Bouquet': 58 days; pastel orange heads; the orange color is from carotene; sunlight intensifies the color, so blanching is not recom-

mended; available from Johnny's Selected Seeds

'Purple Cape': rich purple heads with excellent flavor; hardy; carried by Bountiful Gardens

'Sicilian Purple': 85 days; deep purple, large heads; turns bright emerald green when cooked; available from Nichols Garden Nursery

Kale

Cold weather intensifies the colors of these kales.

'Lacinto': 70 days; blue-green strap leaves, tender; available from Shepherd's

'Nagoya Garnish Red': 60 days; ornamental kale; frilly leaves with red centers and green edges; available from Johnny's Selected Seeds and Harris Seeds and Nursery

'Red Russian': 55 days; tender, frilly gray-green leaves with red veins; withstands summer heat

'Red Peacock': 60 days mature; ornamental kale; red center; feathery leaves; excellent for baby salad greens; 'White Peacock' is a white version; both available from Johnny's Selected Seeds

Kohlrabi

'Kolibri': 55 days; hybrid, purple-skinned kohlrabi, crunchy, sweet flesh; heat tolerant

'Purple Vienna': purple bulbs; old favorite; available from Landreth

Red Cabbage and Flowering Cabbage

'Lasso': 75 days; open pollinated; firm, bright red-purple, good tasting

'Purple Vienna' kohlrabi *(above);* 'Red Fire Dance' cabbage *(below)*

heads; early; available from Garden City Seeds and Pinetree Garden Seeds

Miniature Flowering Cabbage, Tokyo Series: showy 12-inch heads; pink, white, and red, with green edges; cold resistant; available from Nichols Garden Nursery

'Red Drumhead': red Savoy-type cabbage; sweet crinkled leaves; hardy, widely adaptable; available from Seeds of Change and Bountiful Gardens

'Rougette': 80 days; red French variety; 3 pound heads; available from The Gourmet Gardener

'Ruby Perfection': 80 days; purple cabbage with great taste; available from The Cook's Garden

How to prepare: The purple pigments in the cabbage family are anthocyanins and in many cases are not stable when cooked. In particular, the purple in broccoli, cauliflower and kale turns green. However, if not cooked too long, red cabbage and Brussels sprouts can be colorful, especially if vinegar, lemon juice, or as is popular in much of Europe, red wine are added. With the addition of an acid they go from purple to a lovely bright magenta (see the discussion on acids and anthocyanins in "The Chemistry of Cooking" on page 60, and the recipe for Braised Red Cabbage on page 76). If cooked too long, however, both red cabbage and Brussels sprouts turn a dull red-gray.

To keep its color best, use the young leaves of kale raw in salads or as a garnish. Mature leaves are best cooked but lose purple coloring.

The purple pigments in broccoli, cauliflower, and kohlrabis turn green when cooked. To preserve their color, use them raw in salads and with dips. Romanesco broccoli keeps its lovely chartreuse color and the light orange cauliflower varieties stay colorful as well, as long as neither is overcooked.

CARROTS
Daucus carota var. sativus

'Nutri-Red,' 'Danvers Long,' 'Sweet Sunshine,' and 'Belgium White' *(above)*; 'Long Orange' and 'Red Surrey' *(below)*

ANCIENT CARROTS CAME FROM Afghanistan and the roots were mainly purplish or red. Our familiar orange-colored carrots are relative newcomers having been bred in Holland in the 1600s.

How to grow: Plant carrots in early spring as soon as your soil has warmed, or plant late summer for a fall crop. Cultivate and loosen the soil 1 foot deep to make room for the roots. Sow seeds 1/2 inch apart in rows or wide beds and keep the seed bed evenly moist. Thin to 2 inches. In most parts of the country, once sprouted, carrots are easy to grow. When the plants are about 3 inches tall, fertilize with fish emulsion.

Once the seedlings are up, protect plants from slugs. In the upper Midwest, the carrot rust fly maggot tunnels its way through carrots. Floating row covers and crop rotation help. Alternaria blight and cercospora blight can also be a problem.

Most carrot varieties are ready for harvesting when they are at least 1/2 inch across and starting to color (except in the case of white carrots). The optimal time to harvest carrots is within a month after they mature, less in warm weather. Harvest when the soil is moist to reduce breaking off the roots in the ground.

Varieties
'Belgium White' ('White Belgium'): 75 days; white roots with green shoulders; 10 inches long; productive; in cool weather these carrots have a sweet, carroty flavor; in hot weather the flavor becomes too strong and "soapy"; best when eaten cooked

'**Dragon**': 75 days; red-to-purplish exterior, yellow to orange interior; sweet, spicy flavor; the purplish exterior is high in anthocyanin; available from Garden City Seeds

'**Lubina**': 70 days; bright yellow-gold with green shoulders; hearty, sweet flavor; vigorous grower; available from Garden City Seeds

'**Nutri-Red**': 118 days; deep-red carrot; high in lycopene, a precursor to beta-carotene; tastes best cooked

'**Sweet Sunshine**': 72 days; striking true yellow; tender, extra-sweet, 7 inch carrots; available from Burpee

How to prepare: The yellow and orange colors of carrots are carotenoids and are quite stable when cooked. In contrast, the purple pigments in purple carrots, because they are anthocyanins turn an unappetizing gray. To take advantage of the color and the extra nutrients in these purplish carrots, enjoy them raw. Serve baby purple carrots whole or cut mature ones into carrot sticks—combining them with the orange and yellow carrots makes a striking plate.

Cook the white, yellow, and red-orange carrots as you would the familiar orange varieties. To accent their colors, combine the different colors julienned on a plate, sprinkled over a salad, on a dip platter, or as baby cooked carrots with a vinaigrette or herb butter. Carrots, if peeled or grated and thus exposed to the air, eventually turn brown; sprinkle with lemon juice or vinegar to prevent discoloring or add your vinaigrette immediately to stop the oxidation.

CELERY
Apium graveolens var. dulce

RED CELERY HAS BEEN GROWN for many years and is fairly popular in England. Golden celerys are enjoyed in Asia.

How to grow: Celery is a cool-season vegetable that grows best in the spring or fall, or as a winter crop in warm-winter areas. Celery needs full sun (or partial shade in hot areas) and a highly organic soil that drains quickly. Start celery indoors 10 weeks before planting outdoors. Germination takes up to 20 days. After the weather has warmed to the upper 50s (Fahrenheit), move seedlings into the garden and place them 1 foot apart in all directions. Celery requires applications of fish fertilizer every four weeks and a continually moist soil—an organic mulch is helpful. Celery takes 3 to 4 months to mature.

Parsleyworms (the caterpillar of the eastern black swallowtail butterfly), carrot rust fly maggots, and carrot weevil larvae feed on celery. If they are a problem, protect plants with floating row covers. Celery may be afflicted with early blight fungus a disease that grows and spreads in cool, damp weather. Yellows, another disease, is spread by leafhoppers. Practice crop rotation, and rid the garden of all diseased plant residue over the winter.

Some gardeners elect to garden-blanch their red celery. When you blanch celery it becomes less stringy but much lighter in color and contains

'Red Celery' *(above);* 'Chinese Golden' celery *(below)*

35

fewer nutrients. To blanch: after the plants start to mature, exclude light by wrapping the stalks with burlap or straw, surround the bundles with black plastic, and then tie them with string.

Celery is harvested as soon as the stalks are large enough to pull off. New stalks will continue to form from the plant's center, and thus harvesting can be continuous. Or harvest the whole head by cutting the plant off at the ground with a sharp knife.

Varieties

'Chinese Golden': 60 days, small leaves, tender narrow stalks; available from Evergreen Y. H. Enterprises

'Golden Self-Blanching': 115 days; a popular, open-pollinated, early, dwarf variety with pale gold color; available from Seeds Blüm and Bountiful Gardens

'Red': has bronzy-colored green stalks until the frost brings out the dark red color; a splendid variety with very solid heads; cold tolerant; stays fairly red when cooked

How to prepare: The red pigments in red celery are anthocyanins. To preserve the color, use it raw on a crudities platter, for dips, and for stuffing with flavored soft cheeses. Red celeries often need to have the strings removed before serving them. Gold celery keeps its color and can be used raw or cooked.

Pink chard

CHARD
(Swiss chard, leaf chard)
Beta vulgaris var. flavescens

THE NEW STAINED-GLASS COLORS of chard promise to add real pizzazz to the garden and lots of color to the table.

How to grow: Chard can be grown in a vegetable garden but it is equally at home in a flower border. When planting the color mix start the seeds in flats and choose the color of plants you want by waiting until the seedlings are a few inches tall and show their colors.

Swiss chard tolerates a lot more heat than most greens and is moderately hardy. Start in early spring or late summer for mild-winter areas. Plant chard seeds $1/2$ inch deep, 6 inches apart, and thin to one foot. Plant in full sun and neutral soil with lots of added organic matter. For tender succulent leaves, keep plants well watered. Mulch with a few inches of organic matter. When

plants are about six weeks old, fertilize with $1/2$ cup of balanced organic fertilizer for every 5 feet of row.

A few pests and diseases bother chard, mainly slugs and snails (especially when the plants are young), and leaf miner, a fly larvae.

To harvest chard, remove the outside leaves at the base; tender new leaves keep coming throughout the season.

Varieties

'Bright Lights': 55 days; a mix of vividly colorful plants with stems and midribs of red, gold, orange, purple, white, pink—and tender leaves from green to bronze; mild flavor

'Ruby Red' ('Rhubarb'): 60 days; solid red (sometimes dark pink) stems and midribs, and dark green leaves

How to prepare: The pigments in chards are the same as in their close cousin beets—namely betacyanins for the red, and betaxanthins for the gold colors. These pigments are fairly stable if not cooked very long. One caveat:

cut raw chard stems oxidize and soon turn brown if not treated with an acid solution such as a vinaigrette or citrus juice.

For the brightest colors use the chard stems raw. For example, just before serving, julienne the stems of different colored chards into matchsticks and sprinkle them over a winter salad in place of the usual red cabbage. Or pickle the stems and serve them as a relish with roasted meats or mushrooms (recipes, page 66). You can also use the colorful leaves to garnish platters and large salad bowls. Young chard stems can be stuffed with cheese mixtures as you would celery.

Colorful chards can also be added to traditional chard tarts (recipe, page 87) and the leaves can be stuffed with a risotto stuffing and steamed.

Stalks of 'Bright Lights' chard *(top);* 'Ruby' chard *(above left);* closeup of the leaf of ruby red chard *(above, right)*

CORN (MAIZE, INDIAN CORN)

DENT CORN
Zea mays var. indentata

POPCORN
Z. m. var. everta

SOFT CORN (FLOUR CORN)
Z. m. var. amylacea

SWEET CORN
Z. m. var. saccharata

CORN HAS MANY DIMENSIONS. In simple terms, sweet corn is the one that bears those luscious ears we smother with butter; dent and soft corns are used primarily for grinding into corn meal or corn flour; dent varieties are also used as roasting ears; and popcorn for popping.

How to grow: Corn requires summer heat and full sun and is best sown directly in the garden. Corn pollen is transferred by the wind, from the male flower (the tassel) onto the pistil of the female flower (the silk). If corn is planted in long single rows, the silks won't be well pollinated. Instead plant corn in a block of shorter multiple rows, at least four rows deep. Plant seeds in rich soil, 1 inch deep, 4 inches apart; thin to 1 foot apart.

Fertilize sweet corn with organic nitrogen fertilizer at planting time and when plants tassel (when the flower stalks produce pollen). Grinding corns are lighter feeders and more drought tolerant than the sweet corns. With all corn, however, extra water is needed at tasseling time, to guard against poorly filled out ears.

'Hopi Blue' corn

Birds steal seeds out of the ground so cover newly planted seeds with floating row covers until 1 foot tall. The most common insect pests are corn earworms. Other insect pests include corn borers; southern corn rootworms; corn flea beetles, and seed corn maggots. The most common corn diseases are Stewart's bacterial wilt, root rot, corn smut, and southern corn leaf blight.

Sweet corn is ready to eat when the silks are dry and brown and the ears are well filled out. Test for ripeness by tasting a few kernels. Grinding corns and popcorn should be left on the plant until the kernels are dry. If the weather is very wet, cut the stalks after the husks begin to turn brown; store them in a dry place. When the corn is completely dry—which can take weeks— husk the ears and store them in a dry place, or remove the kernels and store them in sealed jars.

Varieties

Some colored varieties of dry corn will be white in the milk stage and only color up when ripe.

Sweet Corn

'Ruby Queen': 75 days; deep red, 8-inch-long ears; sweet, tender kernels; available from Burpee

Grinding Corns

'Bloody Butcher': 100 days; dent corn, large ears of red kernels; makes pink cornmeal; plants grow to 12 feet; available from Fox Hollow Seeds and Seeds Blüm

'Hopi Blue' ("Sakwa-pu"): 90 days; flour corn with blue kernels; ground use for blue cornbread;

drought tolerant; available from Redwood City Seed Company, Native Seed/SEARCH

Popcorn

'Strawberry': 80–110 days; small, deep red ears, to 3 inches long and strawberry-shaped; plants 5 feet tall; resistant to corn earworm; available from Fox Hollow Seeds and The Cook's Garden

How to prepare: The red color in 'Ruby Queen' is from anthocyanin and the color fades and changes unless you microwave it. Serve it as you would any sweet corn or after microwaving it, cut it off the cob and sprinkle the kernels over tacos (recipe, page 85), salads, and chowders. Use 'Strawberry' popcorn as you would regular popcorns (it pops up white). Anthocyanins are also the pigments in blue corn. Use the grinding corns for corn meal as you would in most recipes (See the recipes on pages 88–89). Have some fun experimenting. 'Bloody Butcher' makes a very flavorful red-flecked cornbread. You can use 'Hopi Blue' for bread that retains its bluish-purple color when baked in blue cornbread and blue tortillas (though it usually gets a greenish-hue from the baking powder). Combining 'Hopi Blue' cornmeal with white flour makes a bluish-gray pie crust with a nutty crunch.

If you have only small amounts of corn, grind dry corn in a hand-powered grain mill. For larger amounts of corn, it's possible to purchase grain-grinding attachments to fit popular models of stand mixers.

'Bloody Butcher' corn growing in my garden *(above)*, and a closeup of the corn kernels, *(below)*

CUCUMBERS
Cucumis sativus

CUCUMBERS ARE AN ANCIENT
vegetable that originated in India.

How to grow: Cucumbers are
warm-season annuals and tolerate no
frost. Plant the seeds when the soil and
weather are warm, about 1 inch deep,
6 inches apart in rows. Thin to 2 feet
apart. Cucumbers grow on vines and
are grown on trellises put in place at
the time of planting.

Cucumbers need rich, humus-filled
soil and ample water during the growing season. Work bone meal and blood
meal into the soil before planting. If
plants are pale, apply fish emulsion.

Young cucumber plants are susceptible to cutworms and snails, and
striped and spotted cucumber beetles
can destroy young vines as well as
carry serious diseases. Powdery mildew
is a common problem, particularly late
in the season. More serious diseases are
mosaic virus, scab, and anthracnose;

pull up affected plants as there is no
cure for any of these conditions.

Harvest cucumbers when they are
young and firm but filled out. For best
eating, pick lemon cucumbers when
about the size of a lime and don't let
them get too yellow. Pick white
cucumbers when about 5 inches long
and ivory white. Harvest regularly and
pick off all overripe or damaged fruits
or when plants stop production.

Varieties
'**Lemon**': 65 days; round, yellow fruits;
mild flavor; drought- and rust-resis-
tant plants

'**White**': 60 days; crisp, slicing cucumber with white skin and flesh; skin
eventually turns yellow-orange;
available from Landis Valley and
Seed Savers Exchange

How to prepare: Use cucumber
slices raw as you would green cucumbers. To emphasize the colors try alternating green, white, and yellow
cucumbers on the top of a salad or
buffet plate.

Many variations of eggplant colors

EGGPLANTS
Solanum melongena var.
esulentum, S. integrifolium

EGGPLANTS ARE GENERALLY
purple but there are pink, white,
green, and red varieties as well.

How to grow: Eggplants are tender
perennials grown as annuals. They tolerate no cold. Start seeds indoors 6
weeks before the average date of your
last frost. The seeds germinate best at
80°F. Plant the seeds ¼ inch deep, in
flats. When all danger of frost is past
and the soil has warmed, transplant
into the garden 24 inches apart and
water well. Grow eggplants in full sun,
in rich well-drained garden loam that
has added nitrogen. To increase yield
and to keep the plants healthy, feed
them about three times during the
growing season with fish emulsion. If
you are growing eggplants in a cool cli-

'White' cucumber

'Snowy White' eggplant

mate, cover the soil with black plastic to retain heat. Eggplants need moderate watering.

Flea beetles, spider mites, and whiteflies can be a problem. Flea beetles often appear early in the season, right after transplanting. Spider mites can be a nuisance in warm, dry weather. Nematodes are sometimes a problem in the South. Verticillium wilt and phomopsis blight are common disease problems in humid climates.

Eggplant is ready to harvest when the skin is full-colored but has not yet begun to lose any of its sheen. Press down on the eggplant with your finger, if the flesh presses in and bounces back, it is ripe.

Varieties

'**Asian Bride**': 70 days; white skin streaked with lavender; to 6 inches long, 1 ¹/₂ inches diameter; creamy flesh; productive, lavender flowers; available from Shepherd's

'**Rosa Bianca**': 75 days; large, rose-lavender and white fruit with creamy flavor; one of the most beautiful eggplants, productive; available from Shepherd's

'**Snowy White**': 70 days; pure white color and great eating quality; 5 inches long, 2 ¹/₂ inches diameter; early; available from Shepherd's

'**Turkish Italian Orange**': small orange-red fruits; 4 feet tall, spineless plants; high yielding; available from Southern Exposure

'**Violette De Firenze**': 80 days; spectacular, Italian; large oblong lavender fruits, often with wide white stripes; available from The Cook's Garden

How to prepare: The color of these eggplants will be enjoyed most in the garden, because in preparation the skin is either peeled off or discolors when cooked. Even though the skin changes color, eggplants are wonderful grilled on a barbecue along with other colorful vegetables. Use these colorful eggplants as you would the purple ones in stews, stir-fried, grilled in sandwiches, and pureed with garlic for a dip.

HUÀUZONTLI
Chenopodium nuttaliae

THE BUSHY SPEARS OF THIS TALL plant's seed heads are edible and used in Mexico as a pot herb.

How to grow: Huàuzontli is an annual plant that is started from seed in spring and grows to 3 feet in height. Keep the plant fairly moist during the growing season. In autumn its leaves turn red.

How to prepare: The mild-tasting shoots are eaten like spinach. Traditionally, shoots covered with seed heads are blanched in boiling water; then small bunches are put together with cheese, dipped in egg batter, and fried. According to Craig Dremman of Redwood City Seed Company, it looses little of its fall red color if cooked briefly.

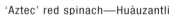

'Aztec' red spinach—Huàuzantli

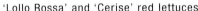

'Lollo Rossa' and 'Cerise' red lettuces

'Rouge d'Hiver' red romaine *(above)*; Red and Green Oak leaf lettuces *(below)*

LETTUCE
Lactuca sativa

RED LETTUCES ARE ESPECIALLY showy in the garden and can be interplanted among flowers.

How to grow: Lettuce is a cool-season annual crop. Most will go to seed or become bitter rapidly once hot weather arrives. In warm weather, lettuce grows better with afternoon shade. In mild-winter areas, lettuce will grow through the winter.

Lettuce prefers soil high in organic matter, needs regular moisture, and profits from light feedings of fish fertilizer every few weeks. Sow seeds 1/8 inch deep outdoors, start seeds indoors in flats, or buy transplants. You can start lettuce outside as soon as you can work the soil in spring. Plant seeds 2 inches apart and 1/8 inch deep. Keep seed beds uniformly moist until seedlings appear. Thin seedlings to between 6 and 12 inches apart, depend-

ing on the variety. Failure to thin seedlings can result in disease problems.

Protect seedlings from birds, slugs, snails, and aphids with floating row covers and by hand picking pests. Botrytis, a gray mold fungus disease, can cause the plants to rot off at the base. Downy mildew, another fungus, will cause older leaves to get whitish patches that eventually die.

You can harvest lettuce at any stage. Leaf lettuces can be harvested one leaf at a time or in their entirety. Heading lettuces are generally harvested by cutting off the head at the soil line.

Varieties

Most of the following red varieties are carried by The Cook's Garden, Johnny's Selected Seeds, and The Gourmet Gardener.

'Brunia': 62 days; a beautiful red oakleaf; leaves dark green with red-brown; large frilly heads

'Cerise': 30 days baby, 48 days full size; deep red color; good for baby lettuces; matures to an iceberg type

'Impuls': 55 days; intensely red 'Lollo Rossa' type; 6- to 8-inch circular mound of frilled leaves

'Mighty Red Oak': 50 days; bronzy-red oakleaf; to 16 inches across; productive; slow to bolt; available from Burpee

'Red Sails': 52 days: burgundy-red fringed and ruffled leaves: fast growing; heat tolerant; deepens in color as it matures

'Red Salad Bowl' ('Red Oak Leaf'): 50 days; pale red color increases to deep red with maturity; withstands heat well

'Rouge d'Hiver': 60 days; deep red romaine; sow in early fall; if you plant earlier it may bolt prematurely

How to prepare: Red lettuces are higher than their green cousins in anthocyanins. Red lettuces are spectacular when used to line a platter and filled with any type of filling imaginable. They are lovely by themselves with a simple vinaigrette or combined with raspberries or sliced pears. All of these colorful lettuces enhance a mixed salad with their color.

'Red Giant Mustard'

MUSTARD, JAPANESE RED
Brassica juncea var. rugosa

JAPANESE RED MUSTARDS ARE tangy, handsome plants with crinkled, wine-red leaves that are enjoyable as baby greens or when fully mature.

How to grow: Mustards are cool-season crops. Plant seeds $1/4$ inch deep, 2 inches apart in early spring or fall in full sun and rich loam. Thin to 1 foot apart if growing to maturity. Or broadcast the seed in a wide bed and grow for cut-and-come-again baby greens. Water regularly or leaves become too hot to eat. Mulch with an organic mulch. Mustards are occasionally plagued by the pests that bother cabbages (see the "Cabbages" entry). Harvest a few leaves at a time as needed. The younger the mustard leaf, the less bite it has.

Varieties

'Osaka Purple': 40 days; 3-foot plants; purple leaves with white veins; mild; great for baby greens

'Red Giant Mustard' ('Giant Red'): 45 days; purple-red, savoyed leaves; tangy; 4 feet tall; great for baby greens

How to prepare: The pigments in mustards are anthocyanins that fade when cooked. Use the leaves raw in sandwiches and salads—they add zing! Baby mustards are fairly mild; they add texture, color, and a slight tang to mesclun salads. Use mustard leaves sparingly in light salads or pair them with other strong-flavored greens in a hearty fall or winter salad with a rich dressing. Though they'll lose most of their color, enjoy the leaves in omelets or stir-fries.

OKRA, RED

Abelmoschus esculentus
(Hibiscus esculentus)

WITH ITS RED PODS AND STEMS and yellow blossoms, red okra is a showy plant.

How to grow: Okra must have hot weather and full sun. Plant seeds 6 inches apart in warm, organic-filled, well-drained soil; thin plants to 2 feet. Apply fish fertilizer after the pods begin to set and once again midway through the season. Okra requires about 1 inch of water a week. In cool-summer areas, mulch plants with black plastic for extra warmth.

Okra is susceptible to a few pests, namely, Japanese beetles, caterpillars, and stinkbugs. Nematodes, verticillium wilt, and fusarium wilt are occasional problems.

Okra pods are usually best harvested before they are 3 inches long or they become woody and the plants stop producing. Use clippers to cut a pod off at its base.

Varieties

'Burgundy': 49 days; stems, leaf veins, and pods are deep red-maroon; plants average 4 feet; pods stay tender until nearly 8 inches; not very disease resistant; carried by Southern Exposure Seed Exchange and Bountiful Gardens

'Red': 55–65 days; tender, tasty red pods; 5 feet tall, yellow-and-red flowers; carried by Abundant Life Seed Foundation

'Red' okra

'Red Velvet': 60–70 days; scarlet pods, stems, and leaf veins; 5 feet tall; carried by Seeds of Change

How to prepare: Red okra pods turn greenish-brown when cooked but keep their color when pickled. Use red okra pickled and with marinades.

ONIONS, RED

Allium cepa

PINK SCALLIONS

A. cepa

RED ONIONS AND SCALLIONS ARE usually milder than most yellow and white versions.

How to grow: Onions prefer cool weather, particularly in their juvenile stage. They grow best in a neutral, well-drained soil rich in organic matter and phosphorous. They like even watering.

Onions and scallions are generally grown from seeds or sets. For full-size onions, select the right variety for your climate and time of year because bulbs are formed according to day length. Short-day onions bulb when they get 10 to 12 hours of light per day, best for spring planting in southern latitudes. Long-day onions require about 16 hours of sun to bulb and are best for northern areas. Medium-day onions require 12 to 14 hours of light a day and do well in most parts of the country.

Start seeds inside in late winter or sow them 1/4 inch deep outside in spring (or fall in mild climates). Plant them in rows or wide beds. Fertilize onions with a balanced organic fertilizer when plants are about 6 inches tall and are beginning to bulb. Large bulbing onions should be thinned to give each plant adequate room for unhampered development. Use the red onion thinnings as pink scallions.

I enjoy serving pink, pearl-type onions in colorful dishes. Some vari-

Red, yellow, and white onions *(left)*; 'Stockton Red' onions *(above)*

are the onion maggot (a fly larvae) and thrips. Since scallions are harvested at a younger stage, they tend to have fewer problems with these pests.

Harvest scallions just as the bulbs begin to swell by pulling the entire plant out of the ground. Onions may be harvested anytime from the scallion stage to mature bulb formation.

Varieties

Red Onions

Onions may be hotter in one part of the country than in another or when grown in different soil.

'Italian Blood Red Bottle': 120 days; day-neutral; large, red, bottle-shaped onion; tangy; available from Nichols Garden Nursery

'Red Burgermaster': 102 days; long-day; reddish-purple skin; spicy; vigorous; stores well

eties are bred to produce these small onions. You can also produce small onions from large red varieties by forcing them as you would to make your own onion sets. To produce small onions (sets), plant seeds in poor soil and sow the seeds thickly. (I've had success sowing them in a shallow nursery flat.) The crowding and lack of nourishment force the plants to bulb up prematurely. 'Red Weathersfield' is a variety especially suitable for this process. (Don't be tempted to cook with the red onions sets available from the nursery; they have probably been doused with fungicides to prevent them from rotting when planted.)

The most common pests of onions

'Purplette' pink scallions

ORACH
Atriplex hortensis

THIS ATTRACTIVE PLANT HAS green and red cultivars. Unlike most greens, orach tolerates fairly warm weather.

How to grow: Plant orach seeds $1/4$ inch deep in good soil 6 to 8 weeks before the last expected spring frost date. Thin to 18 inches apart if growing to maturity. Or grow orach as a baby cut-and-come-again "green" by planting seeds in wide rows and thinning plants to only a few inches apart. Mulch to conserve moisture, as plants should be kept moist but not soggy. Orach has few pests and diseases.

Start to harvest leaves in about 6 weeks. If kept pinched back, plants will produce until the weather gets hot. They go to seed if not pruned.

Varieties

'Red Orach': 37 days; red leaves; to 6 feet; available from Garden City Seeds and Bountiful Gardens

How to prepare: Harvested leaves add a vibrant pink-purple to mixed salads. They have a mild flavor that's a good foil for strong-flavored greens. Orach is a delicious midsummer spinach substitute but it looses much of its color when cooked.

'Red Torpedo': 75 days; medium-day; deep purple outside, white to pink interior; sweet; available from Pinetree Garden Seeds

'Red Weathersfield': 105 days; for northern growing areas, a large, flat, purplish-red, pungent onion; best known for the production of onion sets; available from Lockhart

'Stockton Red': 188 days; medium-day; less sensitive to day length than most onions; available from The Cook's Garden and Lockhart

Pink Scallions

'Deep Purple': 60 days; very attractive; for spring or summer sowing; available from Johnny's Selected Seeds

'Purplette': 60 days; purple skin, pinkish flesh; if allowed to mature, it forms small pearl onions that turn pastel-pink when cooked or pickled; Johnny's Selected Seeds and Seeds Blüm

How to prepare: The onion's red color comes from anthocyanins that tend to fade when cooked, especially for any length of time. For the brightest colors, use red onions chopped or sliced over green salads and tomato salads, in sandwiches, and in omelets and frittatas. My favorite way to feature the pink onion color is with the small, round baby pearl onions that are pickled; pink, pearl onions or cooked to just tender and served with other colorful vegetables in a vinaigrette. My friend Jesse Cool, chef and owner of Flea Street Café in Menlo Park, California, pickles these little onions in dry vermouth and uses them in martinis.

Enjoy pink scallions as you would any scallions. They are particularly nice served raw on colorful appetizer platters, with dips, and sliced and sprinkled over salads and cream soups.

PEAS, SHELLING

GARDEN PEAS, SOUP PEAS

Pisum sativum

PEAS, EDIBLE-PODDED

SUGAR SNAP PEAS, SNOW PEAS

P. sativum var. macrocarpon

MOST PEAS ARE GREEN, OF course, but there a few colorful podded ones that are fun to try.

How to grow: Pea plants are either short bushes or long, climbing vines. Peas require well-drained, organic soil; full sun; high humidity; and cool weather. They tolerate some frost but do poorly in hot weather. Seeds should be planted 1 inch deep, 4 inches apart, in rows 1 foot apart. Most varieties need some form of support that's best placed at planting time. Peas need only a light fertilizing at midseason, but they benefit from regular and deep watering—1 inch per week is ideal.

Seedlings succumb to slugs, snails, and birds, so it's best to cover them until they are 6 inches high. Control pea weevils by lightly dusting wet foliage with lime.

Ideally, peas should be harvested daily during the mature-pod stage. Harvest snow peas when the pod becomes full size but before the seeds enlarge. Left past maturity, they lose

'Golden Sweet' peas

'Capucijner's Purple Pod' peas

sweetness and their production declines. For dry peas, allow pods to ripen and turn brown on the vine. If the weather is very wet or heavy frosts are predicted, bring the vines into a dry barn or porch to dry.

Varieties

'Golden Sugar': flat snow-pea type of pea with light golden pods; available from Seeds Blüm

'Golden Sweet': 70 days; beautiful, lemon-yellow edible pods; two-tone lavender flowers; harvest for pods or for soup peas; available from the Seed Savers Exchange

'Capucijner's Purple Pod' ('Blue Podded'): 80 days; vining; purple pods and lavender blossoms; best for soup peas; available from Abundant

Life Seed Foundation and the Seed Savers Exchange

How to prepare: Use yellow snow pea pods sliced in salads or whole on a dip platter. They hold their color and make a delightful stir-fry with colorful peppers and carrots. The purple-podded pea is primarily a dry pea, tasty in a creamy winter soup.

PEPPERS

Capsicum spp.

PEPPERS IN THE GARDEN ARE A virtual rainbow unto themselves. There just may be more color variations in peppers than in any other vegetable.

How to grow: Peppers are a warm-weather crop. They cannot tolerate frost and won't set fruit unless the temperature is between 65°F and 80°F. Start seeds indoors in flats eight weeks before the average last frost date. When all danger of frost is past and the weather is warm, transplant seedlings into the garden. Transplant peppers 2 feet apart, in full sun (or partial shade in hot climates). They require deep, rich soil, and regular watering. Peppers are fairly heavy feeders so apply fish fertilizer midseason.

Young pepper plants can fall victim to snails, slugs, aphids, and cutworms. Peppers are occasionally prone to the same diseases and pests that afflict tomatoes, although peppers succumb less often.

When peppers are nearly full size, pick them at any color stage. Cut, rather than pull, peppers from the plant's stem.

Peppers—both sweet and hot—
come in every color but blue

'Golden Bell' peppers

Burpee's Giant Golden

'Pretty Purple' pepper

Varieties

Mail-order suppliers The Pepper Gal, Totally Tomatoes, and Tomato Growers Supply Company carry most of the listed varieties. A number of seed companies carry "rainbow" collections of peppers including W. Atlee Burpee & Co., Park Seed Company, Renee's Garden, and in retail stores.

Sweet Peppers

'Albino' ('White Bullnose'): 80 days; creamy-white a long time before going red-orange

'Chocolate Bell': 75 days; large, dark brownish-red fruits

'Golden Bell': many blocky, golden, thick-walled varieties at your local nursery or in catalogs may be generically labeled as simply 'Golden Bell'

'Golden CalWonder': 72 days; a golden bell type that is TMV resistant

'Gypsy': 60 days; from pale yellow to orange-red; tasty elongated fruits; early; productive; performs well in both hot and cold regions; TMV resistant

'Hungarian Sweet Banana' ('Sweet Banana,' 'Long Sweet Hungarian'): 52 days; yellow to flaming orange; 4 to 7 inches long; cylindrical shaped; dependable, high yields; very ornamental

'Mandarin': 74–78 days; green to red to deep red-orange; flavor is best at orange stage; high yields

'Lilac Bell': 70 days; ivory to lavender to crimson with extended lavender stage; blocky fruits with thick sweet flesh; vigorous plants; TMV resistant

'Purple Beauty': 70 days, green to deep purple to red blocky bell, productive, TMV resistant

'Romanian Rainbow': 60 days; ivory to orange then to red bells, often all three colors are on the plant at one time

'Valencia': 72 days; from green to deep tangerine-orange; large, blocky bell; productive; TMV-resistant

'Yellow Belle': 65–75 days; yellow to yellow-orange to crimson red; 'CalWonder' type; thick flesh; productive and reliable; in southern areas, fully ripe peppers may develop fungus in the seed cavity during hot weather

'Yellow Cheese Pimiento': 73 days; green to yellow to orange; large, squash-shaped fruits

Hot Peppers

'Bolivian Rainbow': 75 days; purple, yellow, and red fruits; purple leaves; tall plant, fruits early; productive; available from Seeds of Change

'Cayenne, Golden': 60 days; dark green to golden; from Renee's Garden

'Long Red Cayenne' ('Long Cayenne'): 75 days; slim, 5-inch-long peppers; very hot

'Purple Cayenne': slim, purple peppers to 5 inches; available from Renee's Garden

'Poinsettia': 90 days; 2-foot plants bear-

Orange peppers—both hot and sweet

POTATOES
Solanum tuberosum

POTATOES GENERALLY HAVE white flesh but there are lovely varieties with blue or red flesh as well.

How to grow: Potatoes prefer cool weather so plant them in the spring as soon as the soil has warmed. Potatoes are generally started by planting pieces of the tuber that contain at least one "eye." Set them out as soon as the ground can be worked in the spring. If hard frosts are expected, protect the young plants with floating row covers. Potatoes are best grown in well-drained, fertile, organic soil. For an easy and large harvest, plant potatoes in a trench 6 inches wide by 6 inches deep. Space tubers about 1 foot apart and cover with 4 inches of soil. As the potatoes begin to sprout, fill the trench with more soil until it is level with the existing bed or taller. For highest production, keep the plants moist. If planted with plenty of finished compost, potatoes generally require little fertilizer.

Colorado potato beetles, flea beetles, and aphids can attack potato foliage; wireworms and white grubs damage tubers. The tuber pests are best controlled by regular crop rotation. In highly alkaline soil potatoes may develop a disease called scab, so raise the soil pH to 6. If a plant shows signs of wilt or viral disease, remove and discard it. When potato foliage has died back, dig tubers from one plant to check the crop for tuber size. To avoid damaging underlying tubers, dig carefully and at some distance from the plant's crown.

ing 2-inch, upright, pointed fruits from green to purple to red; available from Fox Hollow Seeds and W. Atlee Burpee & Co.'s Heirloom Seed catalog

'Pretty Purple': 75–90 days; green to lavender to red fruits; foliage and flowers are purple; available Southern Exposure Seed Exchange

'Variegata': 65 days; green, purple, and red fruits; spectacular dwarf plants; leaves variegated green, white, and purple

How to prepare: Red and orange peppers have more vitamins A and C than the unripe green, ivory, and purple ones. The primary pigments in peppers are various carotenoids that are quite stable when cooked. The purple and lilac peppers, however, must derive their color from anthocyanins because they fade quickly when cooked. I feature the purple peppers by serving them raw in salads and presenting them on dip platters.

To accent the colors of the red, orange, yellow, and white bell peppers, prepare them as containers for dips on a buffet table, or stuff them with risotto or bread stuffings. Also cut them into rings or match sticks to decorate a salad or serving platter. All colors of peppers, raw or cooked, are tasty in combination on pizzas and in frittatas, pasta salad, peperonata, and tacos. They are delicious pickled, roasted, and marinated in olive oil, and are splashy and tasty garnishes.

Roast and puree the cooked red and orange peppers and use them in cream soups or sauces. These colorful peppers also can be dried and ground to make different colors of either hot or sweet "paprikas"; sprinkled on potato salads, cream soups, and stuffed baked potatoes; and blended into soft cheeses. For an unusual and healthy appetizer, mix the paprika with salt and dip slices of jicama or white baby turnips into the spicy mixture.

'All Blue' and 'All Red' Potatoes in a harvest with many types of white potatoes.

Varieties

Becker's Seed Potatoes and Ronniger's Seed & Potato Company are mail-order sources specializing in potatoes; they carry both varieties.

'All Blue' ('Purple Marker'): more than 80 days; purple-blue flesh; medium-sized potatoes good for mashing, steaming, and baking

'All Red': more than 80 days; brilliant red skin and pink flesh; medium tubers; good for steaming and boiling

How to prepare: While the pigments in these colorful potatoes are primarily anthocyanins, the deep blue potatoes particularly can be coaxed to keep much of their color. However, if you start with pale blue or very light pink potatoes, the finished dish will probably have little or no color—or in the worst case, turn an unappetizing gray. To retain as much color as possible, boil potatoes with a little vinegar or lemon juice in the water; or microwave them until they are just tender (over-cooking fades the color). To feature the blue and pink varieties in salads, use colorless vinaigrettes instead of creamy dressings. Adding acidic ingredients like vinegar or citrus juices changes the color. The blue potatoes become a bright, deep, magenta-purple; the pink ones turn more red. Combine these dramatic potato slices with yellow and green zucchini, red and orange bell peppers. Top with a spicy dressing—and Olé!—an instant fiesta dish.

While colorful potatoes are interchangeable with white potatoes in most recipes, potato salads (recipe, page 75), lavender or pink mashed potatoes, and vichyssoise (recipe, page 65) are among the most successful presentations.

Caution: Dispose of all portions of a tuber that show any green coloration; they are toxic.

51

RADISHES
Raphanus sativus

'Easter Egg,' 'French Breakfast,' and 'Sparkler' radishes

I'M INCLUDING TWO TYPES OF colorful radishes. The standard European types are usually red but they also come in purple, white, and pink. Asia is the home of a type of daikon called "beauty heart" radishes. Large with colorful pink or green flesh, "beauty hearts" are especially popular in northern China.

How to grow: Standard radishes grow easily and can be planted after the last frost in spring and again in early fall. The "beauty hearts" are a bit more difficult to grow. The resulting roots are quite variable; some have deep color and others remain pale. The Asian radishes are best planted in August in cold-winter areas and from September through December in mild-winter areas for fall and winter harvests.

Plant all radish seeds directly in the garden $1/2$ inch deep. Thin the standard radishes to 2 inches and the beauty hearts to 8 inches. All radishes can be planted in rows or wide beds. The soil should be light and well-drained with a generous dose of compost. Radishes are light feeders so they need little fertilizer. Keep the young radishes constantly moist to avoid cracking and a "too-hot" taste.

In some areas of the country, radishes are bothered by root maggots, a pest best controlled by rotating crops. Flea beetles also can be a considerable problem.

Generally, standard radishes mature within 30 days. They're best harvested

when about the size of cherries—$3/4$ inch in diameter—or 1 inch across for the long, narrow type, usually within 30 days. "Beauty hearts" take about 2 months to mature and are ready when they have reached full size. In cool weather, they can be left in the ground for weeks. Insulate radishes with straw if a hard freeze is expected. If left in the ground too long, short-season radishes have a tendency to get hot and fibrous.

Varieties

Short-Season European Radishes

'Easter Egg': 28 days; flavorful and crunchy; produces a mixture of purple, lavender, pink, and white radishes

'Plum Purple' ('Purple Plum'): quick growing; with deep purple skins and crisp, white flesh; heat tolerant; available from The Cook's Garden

'Easter Egg' radishes

Long-Season Asian Radishes

'Chinese Misato Rose Flesh': 65 days; mild; 4-inch round roots; creamy outside and rosy pink inside; stores well; available from Park Seed Company

'Green Meat': usually ready about 60 days after sowing; 10-inch root with white skin and green flesh; available from Evergreen Y. H. Enterprise

'Misato Green': usually ready about 60 days after sowing; for autumn and winter crops; cylindrical Chinese radish with green flesh; juicy and sweet; easier to grow than the red beauty hearts; available from Nichol's Garden Nursery

'Shinrimei': The name translates to "beauty heart;" Chinese round radish with white skin, green shoulders, and red flesh; needs some late-summer heat to grow well; available from Evergreen Y. H. Enterprises

How to prepare: Serve standard radishes sliced raw in salads, as garnishes, on hors d'oeuvre platters, and with butter on bread or crackers (see the radish salad recipe, page 71). The pink color from anthocyanins fades when cooked. The "beauty heart" radishes are traditionally carved into flowers like water lilies, peonies, and chrysanthemums and are beautiful garnishes on buffet dishes. Crisp and succulent, they are often enjoyed raw—frequently julienned to show off their colors. Sometimes they are sprinkled lightly with sugar. They're also served western style with a light herb dressing or cut into fancy shapes for a dip platter.

'Gold Rush' and 'Sunny Delight' squash

SQUASH, SUMMER
Cucurbita pepo var. melopepo

SUMMER SQUASHES ARE COLORFUL additions to your garden and your table.

How to grow: Squashes are warm-season annuals. In short-summer areas, start seeds indoors. Transplant into hills about 3 feet across and 5 feet apart, placing 3 plants to a hill. Squash needs rich humus soil, full sun, and ample water during the growing season. They also benefit from regular applications of a balanced organic fertilizer that is not too high in nitrogen. Keep young plants well-weeded and don't let them dry out.

Squash may be afflicted with squash bugs as well as the spotted and the striped cucumber beetles. East of the Rockies, squash vine borers can be a problem. Mildew is the most common disease so expect it by season's end.

Pick summer squash when it's quite young and tender; or in its "adolescent" stage when the blossoms have just withered, indicating that the squash is still tender but has developed its flavor; or when it is more mature but still tender. Harvest the fruits regularly, or the plant drastically slows its production.

Varieties

'French White': 50 days; bush; white zucchini with mild flavor; firm meat with few seeds; available from Nichols Garden Nursery

'Gold Rush': 52 days; delicious golden zucchini on a vigorous plant

'Golden Dawn II': 45 days; golden zucchini; uniform fruits; productive plants; high in lutein; available from Garden City Seeds

Yellow and pale green pattypan squash

TOMATOES
Lycopersicon esculentum

CURRANT TOMATOES
L. pimpinellifolium

'Big Rainbow,' 'Green Zebra,' 'Green Grape,' and 'Yellow Brandywine' tomatoes

NO RAINBOW GARDEN WOULD be complete without tomatoes—red, orange, yellow, gold, white, and green.

How to grow: Tomatoes are heat-loving plants. Though perennials, tomatoes are grown as warm-weather annuals as they cannot tolerate frost. Extreme heat can sunburn the fruit, though, so it is necessary to protect them in extremely hot climates. Many varieties, especially the big heirloom, beefsteak types, do not set fruit well in temperatures higher than 96°F or lower than 50°F. Start plants from seed about six weeks before the last average frost date; sow seeds ¼ inch deep in good potting soil. Keep seedlings in a very sunny window or under grow lights. Transplant seedlings when they are about 6 inches tall and after there's any danger of frost. Place plants in full sun, about 4 feet apart in well-drained soil amended with a lot of organic matter. Place the transplants deep; the soil should reach the first set of new leaves. Stake or trellis plants to save space and keep the fruit from spoiling on the ground. After transplanting and again when the fruit begins to set, fertilize tomatoes with fish meal, chicken manure, or a premixed, organic fertilizer formulated for tomatoes. Be careful not to apply excess nitrogen fertilizer, as it favors leaf growth at the expense of the fruit. A form of calcium is often needed to prevent blossom-end rot. If you have acidic soil, adding lime may be necessary every few years because tomatoes prefer a soil pH of about 6.5. Water mature plants infrequently but deeply. Mulch with compost after the soil has warmed thoroughly.

Major pests that afflict tomatoes include tomato hornworms, cutworms, tobacco budworms, nematodes, and whiteflies. A number of diseases are fairly common to tomatoes; they include fusarium wilt, verticillium wilt, alternaria blight, and tobacco mosaic virus. Control diseases by rotating crops, planting resistant varieties, and practicing good garden hygiene.

Harvest tomatoes as they ripen. A rich color and a slight give to the fruit indicate ripeness. Harvest with a slight twist of the wrist or with scissors or shears.

'Sunburst': 50 days; beautiful, bush-type plant with vivid golden, scalloped pattypan squashes; high in lutein, squashes are mild and tender; available from Nichols Garden Nursery

'Sunny Delight': an improved 'Sunburst'-type; golden, scalloped pattypan

How to prepare: The skins of most summer squash are high in lutein. For maximum nutrition, harvest summer squash while they're quite young so the skins don't need to be peeled. Slice them raw for salads or for dipping or serve them grilled with a tasty marinade or stuffed and baked. Mix the yellow and white varieties with the dark green varieties to feature the contrast of colors in cooked dishes (recipe, page 78). Grilled baby squash with their flowers intact are an exquisite treat when served with a marinade or sauce.

Varieties

Medium to Large Tomatoes

Most of the following recommended varieties are available from Tomato Growers Supply Company and Totally Tomatoes.

ps36912: a new variety that is very orange; bred to contain more lycopene and more beta-carotene than other varieties; look for it soon (with a fancy name) from the breeders, Seminis Seeds

'Big Rainbow': 90–100 days; indeterminate; bicolored, beefsteak-type fruit weighing 2 pounds or more; golden orange fruits with ruby red radiating from the blossom end; sweet and meaty; 'Pineapple, Georgia Streak,' and 'Striped German' are very similar varieties

'Caro Rich': 80 days; determinate; slightly flattened, 5- to 6-ounce, deep orange fruits have ten times the provitamin A as other tomatoes

'Cherokee Purple': 72 days; short vines; unusually colored purplish, red-brown tomato; full of flavor; available from Southern Exposure Seed Exchange

'Green Zebra': 75 days; indeterminate; 2-inch amber-green fruits with darker green stripes; light green flesh

'Italian Gold' VF: 70 days; determinate; a golden 'Roma' paste tomato, pear-shape; compact plants; prolific

'Mandarin Cross': 77 days; indeterminate; succulent 3-inch orange fruits; late to ripen; for gardeners with long growing seasons

'Taxi': 64 days; determinate; early; meaty, 3-inch lemon-yellow fruits; compact plants; available from Johnny's Selected Seeds

'White Beauty' ('Snowball'): 85 days; mild, meaty, creamy white fruits averaging 8 ounces

'Yellow Brandywine': 100 days; indeterminate; yellow fruit with creamy texture; extremes of temperature may cause the fruit shape to vary

'Yellow Stuffer': 76 days; indeterminate; a hollow, yellow tomato perfect for stuffing; tall, productive vines

Cherry Tomatoes

'Green Grape': 70 days; determinate; 1-inch, yellow-green, juicy fruits; short, compact plants

'Sun Gold': 57 days; indeterminate; 1-inch, bright orange fruits with delicious flavor; vigorous plants with long clusters of fruits

'Sweet Gold F1': 60 days; indeterminate; yellow-gold, 1/2-ounce fruits; vigorous and productive vines; available retail from Renee's Garden

'Yellow Pear': 78 days; bite-size, yellow tomatoes shaped like small pears; low in acid; vigorous vines; disease resistant

Currant Tomatoes

Currant tomatoes are huge plants that sprawl and reseed.

'Yellow Currant': 62 days; indeterminate; related to the wild, yellow currant tomato of South America; vines produce hundreds of 1/2-inch, sweet, tart fruit; thick-skinned, disease resistant, hardy; available from Harris

How to prepare: To fully enjoy the different colors of tomatoes, serve them raw. The pigments in tomatoes are carotenoids, however, and are fairly stable when cooked. The red pigment lycopene in tomatoes has been found to lower the risk of prostate cancer.

The large-fruited, gold, red, orange, yellow, purple, and green tomatoes are lovely sliced on the salad plate or on top of a fresh tart (recipe, page 77). They can be cut in wedges and arranged on a platter or around a dip plate or on a pizza. Use the rainbow of colorful cherry tomatoes in salads, with dips, as hors d'oeuvres. Sauté briefly in olive oil and garlic and arrange over cheese toasts (recipe, page 68), on a green salad, or in pasta. These colorful little tomatoes can also be dried; they keep much of the color. Try white tomatoes mixed with other colors on a salad plate. Or "mess" with people's minds and make a mystery marinara sauce for pasta (recipe, page 86), or pour a white Bloody Mary.

Top row, from left: 'Mandarin Cross'; 'Yellow Stuffer'; 'Striped Cavern.' *Middle row:* harvest of 'Taxi,' 'Yellow Pear,' and 'Caro Rich' tomatoes; 'White Beauty'; mix of cherry tomatoes. *Bottom row:* Harvest of orange tomatoes; 'Yellow Pear'; 'Sungold'

WATERMELON
Citrullus lanatus

WATERMELON FLESH CAN BE red, orange, yellow, peach, even white.

How to grow: For general growing information about watermelons, see the "Cucumber" entry on page 40. Melons are more sensitive to cool conditions than cucumbers, so in cool-summer areas use a black plastic mulch to raise the soil temperature. Reduce watering toward harvest time; too much water then results in insipid fruits and split melons.

Watermelon is ripe when the fruit's surface skin is dull, tough, and difficult to puncture with your fingernail; the bottom of the melon has changed from green to yellow; and the tendrils on the stem near the fruit are brown.

Varieties

'Moon and Stars': 100 days; to 30 pounds, pinkish-red flesh, fine flavor; leaves and green rind are covered with golden splotches (moons) and small gold speckles (stars)

'New Orchid': 80 days; 8 to 10 pounds, bright orange flesh; available from Johnny's Selected Seeds

'New Queen': 75 days; orange flesh; 6 pounds; spreads to 9 feet; a 1999 All American selection; available from Park Seed Company

'Yellow Doll': 68 days; crisp, sweet, yellow flesh; oval, 4 to 7 pounds

How to prepare: Lycopene is one of the carotenoids that gives watermelon its red color. The lovely yellow, orange, and red flesh of watermelons lends

itself to endless colorful party dishes. Create sunset salads with cubes of red, orange, and yellow melons drizzled with a sweet lime dressing. Make them into margaritas—cubes stacked in a goblet and sprinkled with a mixture of lime, sugar, and tequila. Arrange colorful melon balls in a buffet fruit salad or a rainbow of watermelon cubes sprinkled with a spicy Thai mixture of roasted peanuts, chilies, *nam pla* (a fish sauce used like soy sauce), and cilantro. Lay out different colors of watermelon slices or strips on platters to create a color shift from yellow to orange to red or stand them up around the edges of a crystal bowl filled with crab salad.

'New Queen' *(above)*, 'Yellow Doll' and 'Tiger Baby' icebox watermelons *(below)*

cooking from the rainbow garden

I've been attracted to vegetables of unusual colors for as long as I can remember. As a gardener I enjoy both their novelty and beauty and as a cook I glory in their eye appeal. And why not? A plate of sliced red, orange, and yellow tomatoes becomes an artistic creation. Further, red, orange, and yellow bell peppers not only look more exciting than green peppers, they taste much better too. Then there's the fact that I'm a "show-off" cook. Through the years I found I could set guests atwitter when serving pureed 'All Blue' potatoes or lavender vichyssoise or drizzling margaritas over a melange of red, orange, and yellow watermelon cubes!

My experiences with these colorful varieties were not always positive. Twenty years ago, when I was new to

Red, white, and blue potato salad, a tomato tart of many colors, and rings of bell peppers show the range of colorful dishes that utilize vegetables of many hues.

cooking them, most of the chefs and cookbook authors I knew had never even seen blue potatoes much less prepared them. Fumbling in the dark I would gnash my teeth when the lovely lavender vichyssoise I'd visualized turned into a dismal gray soup (through trial and error I learned to start with only the darkest blue potatoes and to add lemon juice to set the

pigments. See the recipe, page 65). I remember making and refrigerating a chiffonade of orange chard stems in the morning only to find them an unappetizing dull, orange-brown at dinner that night. Then there were all those puzzling results: Why did purple asparagus, beans, and cauliflower turn green when cooked but purple cabbage remained purple? Why did red okra lose its color when cooked but red beets and all the red and orange peppers and tomatoes keep their color?

At first, I gleaned a few answers from Jan Blüm and Renee Shepherd as well as a few chefs. Then, bless Harold McGee. In 1984 he wrote *On Food and Cooking,* a fabulous dissertation about the science of cooking including detailed information about pigments in vegetables. With McGee's information I could more reliably predict how a vegetables' color would hold up in the kitchen.

Basically, there are four major groups of pigments in plants. Each group has different functions in the plant and in the kitchen. The pigment groups are the chlorophylls, the anthocyanins, the carotenoids, and the betalains. Because vegetables often contain more than one pigment, the color of a vegetable can be deceptive. For example, while the orange carotenoids in carrots are obvious, the same orange pigments are masked in dark green leafy vegetables because of large amounts of chlorophyll.

The Chemistry of Cooking

Chlorophylls: We're most familiar with the chlorophylls and their life-giving ability to take the sun's energy and through photosynthesis convert water and carbon dioxide into sugars. Chlorophylls are the green pigments in leaves and vegetables, and they are marginally stable when cooked. While most green vegetables are not the focus of this book, it certainly is most pleasing to be able to cook them well and produce lovely bright green, not khaki-colored, asparagus and broccoli to combine with other colorful vegetables. It helps, therefore, to know that chlorophyll is affected adversely by heat, acids, different metals, and enzymes. For example, long cook times dull the color because the cell

walls break down and the green pigments leak out. Green pigment also degrades when the cook covers the pan so acids from the vegetables deposit on the lid and drip back in the water. To keep the green pigments as bright as possible in green vegetables like beans, peas, and spinach, McGee recommends cooking them as quickly as possible in a large volume of boiling water, uncovered, and for a maximum of seven

minutes. Cut large vegetables in pieces so they cook in the allotted seven minutes. Drain them immediately.

Anthocyanins: Anthocyanins comprise a large family of pigments that give flowers, vegetables, and fruits a range of colors from purple and blue to shades of red. The amount in plants can vary from season to season; for instance, pale red kales and lettuces

The red varieties of basil are a great addition to herbal vinegar, turning it a lovely shade of pink.

usually turn a dark burgundy in cold weather. Anthocyanins are water soluble and the majority fade badly when cooked. I find some anthocyanin pigments more stable than others, even from plant to plant, and I can't always predict their behavior when cooked. This is especially true when these pigments come in contact with acidic and alkaline substances, as anthocyanins are sensitive to pH. The anthocyanin family is so sensitive to pH that they can be used as a rough litmus test. To experience this effect I followed McGee's suggestion: I slivered red cabbage and put half of it in a bowl with a tablespoon of vinegar and the other half in a bowl with two teaspoons of baking soda dissolved in water. As predicted, the vinegar mixture turned bright pink and the baking soda mixture turned a lovely sky blue.

Anthocyanins are the colorful pigments in red cabbage, red mustard, red lettuce, red onions, blue corn, purple basil, purple asparagus, purple artichokes, purple potatoes, purple beans, purple carrots, eggplants, and radishes. (See the individual listings in "The Rainbow Vegetable Encyclopedia" for plant-by-plant details.)

To get the most benefit from the colors, whenever possible I use these vegetables raw. If they need to be cooked, I cook them for as short a time as possible. Some, like purple string beans and asparagus, lose all their purple color and turn green before the vegetable is tender. Others, such as red cabbage and blue potatoes, can be coaxed to keep much of their color, especially if you add lemon juice or

The pigment anthocyanin in red cabbages, basil, and blue potatoes is pH sensitive. They turn blue when put in a baking soda solution *(above)*, and they turn pink in vinegar water. When green vegetables are boiled too long they lose their bright green color. *(below)* Overcooked beans on the left and properly cooked beans on the right.

vinegar. The acid helps preserve the color though they turn from purple to magenta.

Carotenoids: Carotenoids consist of a large group of pigments that play an indirect role in photosynthesis. We see these red, yellow, and orange pigments in sweet potatoes, muskmelons, water-melons, tomatoes, peppers, yellow squash, and carrots. These pigments are fat soluble; when cooked, they keep most of their color. Carotenoids, however, fade if cooked for a very long time or change color at elevated temperatures. For example, red tomatoes turn yellow-orange when cooked in a pressure cooker. All things considered, the carotenoids are a joy for the color-maven cook. As Harold McGee says, "…compared to the green chlorophylls and multihued anthocyanins, the carotenoids are a model of steadfastness."

Betalains: This is another category of pigments found in only one order of plants, the *Chenopodiales*, a classification (order) of plants that includes the genera Beta and Atriplex. The betalains include the compounds betacyanin and betaxanthin. Betacyanin gives red beets, red chard, and red amaranths their color; betaxanthin gives golden beets and orange chard their bright sunset hues. Unlike the anthocyanins, these rosy pigments are fairly stable if cooked briefly. In my experience, pickling seems to make the colors even more stable. Long cooking gives the vegetables a brownish look. As a note, betalains are never found in combination with anthocyanins.

Super-Healthy Vegetables

Pigments and vitamins are related chemicals in vegetables and usually there is a direct correlation between vivid color and their health-giving benefits. The red and orange carotenoids and the blue and red anthocyanins are categorized by scientists not only as pigments but also as phytochemicals (plant chemicals), a broad class of thousands of substances derived from plants that can have a beneficial effect on health. Dr. John

Many breeders, such as those at Seminis Seeds, are introducing vegetables with extra nutrition, such as this as-yet-unnamed red-orange carrot with extra beta carotene.

Navazio, a plant breeder with Alf Christianson Seed Company, prefers to call them phytonutrients, and explains, "Most phytonutrients are antioxidants, that is they collect and remove "free radicals" (highly reactive molecules that have the potential to damage our DNA and arteries). These antioxidants also may also boost our immune systems; inhibit attacks from bacteria, fungi, and viruses; and help protect against cancer, premature aging, and age-related blindness." Research indicates that relatively high amounts of these chemicals are needed when compared to vitamins; that some work in combination with other phytochemicals and vitamins; and that while all vegetables and fruits contain phytochemicals, they do so in varying degrees. With the latter in mind, plant breeders like Dr. Navazio are hard at work developing new varieties especially high in these phytochemicals. Look for new, especially colorful (and thus healthful) vegetable varieties to be introduced in the future. See the many available now that are listed in "The Rainbow Vegetable Encyclopedia."

When preparing these extra-nutritious vegetables, it helps to know that raw vegetables usually have the most color when we use them in recipes, but not necessarily the most nutrition. To quote Dr. Navazio, "While some nutrients are lost in cooking, some become more available. For example, light cooking actually increases beta-carotene availability in carrots and lycopene in tomatoes, probably by softening the tissue and making it more digestible." Further, valuable nutrients are lost when some vegetables are peeled. For instance, much of the lutein in squash is located in the skin; when beets are peeled before boiling, nutrients are lost to the water. Another aspect of rainbow cooking involves creating especially colorful meals. Consequently, a platter of vegetables for a rainbow party platter might include slices of pink radishes, yellow zucchini, purple broccoli florets, snap beans, and orange and red cherry tomatoes. What an array of both colors and nutrients! So you can

see, the most eye appeal, can also mean the most nutrition.

Since the 1970s, research about antioxidants as "chemopreventers" has highlighted carotenoids and anthocyanins with their ability to cut down on cardiovascular disease and certain forms of cancer. The latest information indicates that chlorophylls are antioxidants; betalains may be too, but the carotenoids and the anthocyanins are best documented at this time.

Carotenoids: There are dozens of carotenoids in foods, the most familiar being beta-carotene, one of the orange pigments. Its healthful benefits have been known for years as it is the primary source of provitamin A, which our bodies convert to vitamin A. Vitamin A is an essential nutrient required for a healthy immune system, for growth, for reproduction, and to prevent night blindness. More recently research shows beta-carotene also acts as an antioxidant and may lower the risk of several cancers. Evidence also shows beta-carotene works well only when consumed with other carotenoids, not when isolated in pill form. Further, most Americans consume only 1.5 mg a day, far less than the recommended 5 to 10 mg. Beta-carotene is in many vegetables; for instance, a single sweet potato contains 5 to 10 mg. Other vegetables that are great sources of beta-carotene include carrots, leafy greens including beet greens (generally the darker green the leaf the higher the carotenoid content), broccoli, cantaloupe, orange tomatoes, and red peppers. Another carotenoid,

lycopene, lends its red color to watermelon and tomatoes; evidence shows it may help protect against prostate cancer. Yet another carotenoid, lutein, helps prevent damage to the retina as we age; people who consume little lutein are more apt to suffer from macular degeneration. Lutein is a yellow pigment that gives bright color to summer and winter squashes where it is found primarily in the peel. Lutein is present but masked in spinach, beans, and green peppers.

Anthocyanins: The pigments that make many vegetables red, blue, or violet are in a group of cancer-fighting phytochemicals called flavonoids. Anthocyanins are in red cabbage, basil, and lettuce; purple carrots; blue potatoes and corn; eggplants; and radishes. The healthful effects of anthocyanins are less well known than the carotenoids but Dr. Navazio says they also are considered antioxidants that neutralize free radicals that cause cell damage and protect against cardiovascular diseases and certain cancers.

cooking
with
colors

Now that you know the chemistry of cooking colorful vegetables, it's on to creating Technicolor layouts. First some of the basics.

To arrange colorful raw vegetables on a dip plate, try making combinations. Instead of using orange peppers or tomatoes alone, experiment by combining them with red, green, and yellow varieties too. Salads lend themselves to the multicolor approach. Use red orach, ornamental kale, lavender radishes, and any of the vegetables mentioned above. Arrange them on a plate to enhance their many colors or add them to a conventional tossed salad.

If you are serving the vegetables cooked, look for light, transparent dressings to feature the colors best. Dark or opaque sauces and dressings muddy the colors. For instance, roasting red onions with olive oil and balsamic vinegar features the rosy colors better than a cream sauce; blue and red potato salads look best with a vinaigrette instead of mayonnaise. For many more ideas enjoy Renee Shepherd's interview, the multitude of suggestions in "The Rainbow Vegetable Encyclopedia," and the recipes that follow.

These exotic vegetables should inspire your own creations as perhaps no other produce has. Here's a chance to treat your garden as an artist's palette. Make a multicolored quiche, bicolored paprika from orange and yellow peppers, or nestle a rainbow of red, yellow, and green cherry tomatoes among your spaghetti squash strands. I plan to serve a white Bloody Mary

with a swizzle stick of red celery. Someday I would like to bake tricolored cornbread from my red, blue, and yellow grinding corns; one section of the loaf will be pink, one light blue, and the other yellow. Maybe I'll even use one of those cake pans with compartments to separate the batters to make checkerboard cornbread. With a rainbow garden, the sky's the limit.

In a large saucepan, melt the butter and sauté the onions over medium heat till softened but not browned, about 7 minutes. Add the potatoes and 3 cups of water. Cover and simmer until potatoes are tender, 15 to 20 minutes.

Add the lemon juice, half-and-half, and seasonings and puree the soup in a food processor or blender. Chill and serve cold. Garnish by sprinkling the soup with the chives and the chive flowers, separated into florets.

Serves 4.

Golden Gazpacho

This classic Spanish recipe is usually made with red tomatoes and green peppers, but here I put a spin on the ball and make it with gold tomatoes and yellow bell peppers.

7 to 10 medium ripe gold tomatoes

1 large yellow pepper

1 small onion, or 2 to 3 scallions

2 garlic cloves, minced

$1/2$ green Anaheim chile pepper

1 small hot red chile pepper, or to taste

1 large or 2 small cucumbers, peeled

1 tablespoon extra virgin olive oil

$1/3$ cup white wine vinegar

$1/2$ cup dry white wine

Salt and freshly ground black pepper

3 or 4 sprigs fresh cilantro

Garnish: cilantro sprigs, a slice of tomato, or diced avocado

Lavender-Tinted Vichyssoise

Vichyssoise is an elegant but easily made first course. Make it with blue potatoes and you'll really delight your guests. To get the lavender effect you need to use the very deep purple varieties. The medium or light blue potatoes carried by some seed companies will give you a sickly gray, not lavender, soup. Serve this lavender vichyssoise in white or clear glass bowls so the color is featured, garnished with chives and chive florets.

2 tablespoons butter

3 onions, diced (about 3 cups)

3 to 4 deep-blue potatoes, peeled and cubed (about 3 cups)

1 tablespoon fresh lemon juice

1 cup half-and-half

Salt and freshly ground black pepper

Dash of nutmeg

Garnish: fresh chive leaves and flowers

Immerse the tomatoes in boiling water for 30 seconds, or until the skins have loosened. Peel them and remove the seeds and cores. Remove the seeds and membranes from the yellow pepper. Chop the rest of the vegetables coarsely for processing in the food processor or blender (if you use a food processor the soup will have some crunch; using the blender will give a smoother texture).

Process all ingredients in batches, pouring them into a large nonreactive bowl to mix. Refrigerate the soup at least 3 hours before serving. If the gazpacho is too thick, thin it with a little cold vegetable or chicken stock before serving. Taste and adjust seasonings. Serve the soup in individual bowls and garnish each serving as desired.

Serves 4.

1/2 cup diced cooked red beets
     (1 medium beet)
1 tablespoon diced red onion
1/2 teaspoon celery seeds
1/8 teaspoon salt
1 tablespoon honey
1 1/2 cups red wine vinegar

Select a sterilized pint jar that seals well. In the bottom put the peppercorns and cloves. In a small bowl, combine all ingredients except the vinegar and transfer them into the pint jar. Add vinegar until it covers all the ingredients. Screw the top in place and rotate the jar a few times to stir the ingredients. Refrigerate.

To blend the flavors, repeat the rotating process a few times over the next several days. When serving, leave the cloves and peppercorns in the bottom.

Makes about 1 pint.

Golden Chard Relish with Curry

8 pearl onions, peeled
1 cup diced yellow chard stems
     (2 to 3 stems)
1 teaspoon yellow mustard seeds
1/2 teaspoon coriander seeds
1/2 cup white wine vinegar
1 tablespoon honey
1 tablespoon curry powder
1 garlic clove, crushed
Pinch of salt

In the bottom of a sterilized 1 1/2-pint jar with a tight fitting lid, put 4 of the onions. Cover the onions with half of the chard stems. Top the chard with the remaining onions and then fill the jar with the rest of the chard.

Combine the remaining ingredients in a small bowl and mix well. Pour them into the jar and rotate it to stir the ingredients. Refrigerate. Rotate the jar a few times a day for the first few days.

Makes 1 cup.

Two Rainbow Chard Relishes

These two chard relishes are both quite spicy and crunchy, yet have very different flavors. Offer them with poultry or mild fish and with egg dishes. Use them within two weeks.

Ruby Chard Relish with Spicy Beets

1 teaspoon whole peppercorns
1 teaspoon whole cloves
1 1/2 cups diced red chard stems
     (3–4 medium stems)

Pickled Golden Beets

When I was a child, my cousin and I got into big trouble by consuming almost the entire batch of my aunt's pickled beets that she had made for a potluck dinner. We started by sampling them but we just couldn't stop. She used red beets, but I like to use golden beets because they don't bleed all over my plate. I serve these beets as a condiment with a salad or to accompany a sandwich. The pickled beets will last a few weeks in the refrigerator.

> 6 large or 9 medium 'Burpee's
>   Golden' beets
> 1 large sweet white onion, sliced
>   thin
> 1/3 cup sugar
> 1 cup cider vinegar
> Beet juice
> 1 teaspoon mixed pickling spices

Remove all but 1 inch of the greens from the beets. Wash the greens and put them in a large kettle. Barely cover the beets with water, and boil until just tender. (Depending on the size of the beets, this will take 1 hour to 1 hour and 20 minutes). Drain the beets and reserve the liquid. Set them aside to cool. Peel the beets and cut them into thin slices.

In two wide-mouth (pint-size) sterilized mason jars, layer the beets with the onion slices within a half inch of the top. In a saucepan put the sugar, vinegar, about a cup of the reserved beet juice, and the pickling spices and bring to a boil.

Pour the hot pickling mixture over the beets and onions until they are completely covered. (If you run out of pickling liquid, top the jars off with hot beet juice.) Close the jars. Cool them slightly and refrigerate until ready to serve.

Makes 2 pints.

[note]

Pickling spices are a combination of mustard seeds, cloves, cinnamon, peppercorns, hot peppers, celery seeds, and coriander seeds.

Toy Box Cherry Tomatoes with Warm Gruyère Cheese Toasts

Doug Gosling, of the Occidental Arts and Ecology Center in Occidental, California, sold a mix of different cherry tomatoes at farmer's markets for years and called them his Toy Box selection. Jesse Cool, executive chef and owner of Flea Street Café in Menlo Park, California, takes Gosling's colorful concept to the table in the following rustic appetizer.

For the marinated tomatoes:

  2 tablespoons chopped chives
  $1/4$ cup finely chopped parsley
  1 tablespoon finely chopped rosemary
  1 tablespoon finely chopped basil
  $1/3$ cup extra virgin olive oil
  2 garlic cloves, minced
  3 tablespoons balsamic vinegar
  Salt and freshly ground black pepper
  2 pounds (5 to 6 cups) cherry tomatoes of all colors: select from green grape, red cherry, yellow pear, locerno's Ivory Pear, sweet 100, sun gold, and many others

For the Gruyère cheese toasts:

  2 tablespoons extra virgin olive oil
  3 garlic cloves, finely chopped
  4 large slices of thick rustic Italian bread
  4 thin slices Gruyère cheese, $1/2$ ounce each slice

To make the marinated tomatoes: In a large bowl, put the chives, parsley, rosemary, basil, olive oil, and vinegar and mix. Add salt and pepper and stir to combine. Add the tomatoes, cover, and marinate for a minimum of an hour.

To make the toasts: Preheat the broiler. Mix the olive oil with the garlic and let sit 10 minutes. Brush the mixture on one side of each slice of bread. Broil the brushed side until lightly browned. Put a piece of cheese on the raw side of each piece of bread and set the bread aside until the tomatoes are ready.

Just before serving, preheat broiler again if necessary. Lay bread on a rack or cookie sheet and toast under the broiler 2 or 3 minutes or until the cheese has melted.

To assemble, place a slice of still-warm toasted bread on a plate or in a shallow soup bowl. Spoon one quarter of the tomatoes and some of the marinade around each piece of toast.

Serves 4.

Romano Bean Salad with Grilled Tuna

This mid-summer treat is great with crusty bread, and just right for a light fancy lunch.

For the dressing:

1/2 cup extra virgin olive oil

3 to 4 tablespoons fresh lemon
    juice

Salt and freshly ground black pepper

For the salad:

1/2 small red onion, thinly sliced

1 teaspoon salt

1 medium red bell pepper

1 1/2 pounds green and gold
    Romano beans, sliced 1 inch on
    the bias (about 4 cups)

Optional: 3-inch sprig of fresh win-
    ter savory

8 to 10 leaves butter or leaf lettuce

1/2 to 2/3 pound fresh tuna fillet

To make the dressing: In a small bowl, whisk the olive oil, lemon juice, salt, and pepper together until they emulsify and set aside.

To make the salad: Put the onion slices into a small bowl, cover them with cold water, and add the salt. Mix together and let them sit for 1 hour to remove some of the bite.

Meanwhile, roast the pepper over the flame of a gas stove, or under a broiler until charred. Place the charred pepper into a brown paper bag and let it cool. When it is cool enough to handle, remove the seeds, scrape off the skin, and cut the pepper into 1/2-inch strips. Set them aside.

Steam the beans with the (optional) savory over simmering water about 5 minutes or until just tender. Drain the beans, discarding the savory. Shock the beans in ice water until they are chilled and drain again. Drain the onion slices. Arrange the butter lettuce leaves on a serving platter or in a large flat bowl. Arrange the beans, onion slices, and peppers over top.

Meanwhile, preheat the grill. Brush the tuna with one tablespoon of the dressing mixture. Over high heat, grill the tuna to medium rare for about 7 minutes on each side. Cut the fish on the bias into 1/2-inch-thick slices and arrange them on the vegetables. Drizzle the remaining dressing over the tuna and the vegetables. Serve immediately.

Serves 4.

Riot of Color Salad

How about a really colorful salad for a special occasion? Use your imagination and the prettiest edible flowers from your garden.

For the dressing:

> 1 ¹/₂ tablespoons white wine vinegar
> 3 to 4 tablespoons sunflower oil
> 1 tablespoon clover or wildflower honey
> Salt and freshly ground black pepper

For the salad:

> 1 large head romaine lettuce
> 1 head butter lettuce
> 1 small head frisée
> 4 to 6 young leaves of yellow chard
> About a dozen edible flowers such as yellow and blue violas, purple pansies, nasturtiums, yellow calendulas, and red dianthus

To make the dressing: In a small bowl, combine the vinegar, sunflower oil, honey, salt and pepper. Set aside.

To make the salad: Arrange the romaine lettuce, butter lettuce, and chard leaves on a large colorful platter. Separate the flowers into petals, reserving some whole. Sprinkle the greens with flower petals and garnish with the whole blossoms. Bring the salad to the table and let diners dress their own salad.

Serves 4.

Rainbow Party Slaw with Chard

For a party dish this slaw is fairly low in calories. Serve it with grilled vegetables, fish, or as part of a buffet selection.

For the dressing:

Juice of 1 lemon

$2/3$ cup white wine vinegar

1 teaspoon salt

$3/4$ teaspoon celery seeds

$1/3$ cup vegetable oil

3 to 4 tablespoons frozen apple
juice concentrate

Freshly ground black pepper

For the salad:

1 large green cabbage, finely sliced
(about 8 cups)

1 cup thinly sliced chard leaves

2 cups finely sliced carrots (about 4
carrots)

1 small sweet onion, thinly sliced

1 cup thinly sliced red chard stems
(about 4 chard stems)

To make the dressing: In a small bowl, combine the lemon juice, vinegar, salt, celery seeds, oil, apple concentrate, and pepper. Stir until well blended. Set aside.

To make the salad: Place the cabbage in the bottom of a large salad bowl. Creating a decorative pattern, arrange the chard leaves, the carrots, the onions and finally, the chard stems on top of the cabbage.

Pour the dressing over the sliced vegetables and serve. The salad may be refrigerated for a few hours, but the dressing will separate and the red chard stems will lose some of their color if it sits too long.

Serves 8 to 10.

Red, White, and Green Radish Salad

This recipe is another imaginative creation from Renee Shepherd, of Renee's Garden, and Fran Raboff who work together to develop novel recipes.

For the dressing:

1 tablespoon fresh lemon juice

1 tablespoon raspberry vinegar

1 teaspoon stone-ground mustard

1 teaspoon sugar

3 tablespoons extra virgin olive oil

Salt and freshly ground black pepper

For the salad:

2 bunches 'Easter Egg' radishes,
thinly sliced

$1/4$ cup chopped red onions

3 tablespoons chopped fennel leaves

1 fennel bulb, diced

$1/2$ cup thinly sliced scallions,
including part of the green

1 large unpeeled green apple, diced

$1/4$ cup dried currants

Garnish: $1/3$ cup coarsely chopped
toasted walnuts

To make the salad: Combine the dressing ingredients and whisk until blended.

In a salad bowl, combine the radishes, onion, fennel leaves, fennel bulb, scallions, apple, and currants. Pour the dressing over the salad, tossing until mixed. Refrigerate the salad for several hours before serving. Garnish the salad with the chopped walnuts before serving.

Serves 6.

Rainbow Beets Vinaigrette

I like to make this recipe with beets of many colors: gold, red, white, and pink. I steam rather then boil them, so the red and gold beets do not bleed all over the pink and white ones. The greens are delicious too. Steam them separately and they can be served on the same plate with the beets.

6 medium beets, of assorted colors

3 tablespoons balsamic vinegar

$1/3$ cup extra virgin olive oil

$1/2$ teaspoon minced fresh tarragon
or dill

Salt and freshly ground black pepper

Wash the beets and steam them for about 40 minutes, or until they are just tender. Cool then peel and slice them.

In a bowl, put the vinegar, oil, herbs, and seasonings and stir. Pour the dressing over the beets and let them marinate for about 1 hour. Serve hot or cold. Serves 4.

Garden Celebration Salad

This dish is a busy assembly project and takes lots of bowls, but it requires little in the way of technique. It provides plenty of room for creativity and makes a spectacular party salad. Some of the vegetables work best when cooked, others when raw. As with any good garden recipe, the ingredient list is fluid and can be varied by the season and by what's in the garden.

The salad has five layers of colors, each layer with a slightly different flavor combination. Suggested vegetables and herbs for the orange/gold layer include slivered carrots, chopped orange peppers, gold beets, and sliced gold tomatoes; for the yellow layer: yellow zucchini, wax beans, chopped yellow peppers, and sliced yellow tomatoes. For the green layer choose among: chopped lettuces, cabbages, baby spinach, snow pea pods, scallions, and any of the herbs: parsley, chives, basil, fennel, or savory. For the red layer I suggest: red beets, tomatoes, and peppers; and for the purple layer: chopped red cabbage, magenta radicchio, and blue potatoes.

I've given directions for stacking the prepared vegetables in a glass trifle bowl to reveal the colors through the sides of the bowl, but the same ingredients can be laid out on a large colorful platter instead. If you use a clear glass bowl, the moisture from the vegetables will condense on the bowl when you add hot ingredients or when you bring it out of the refrigerator. Let the bowl stand at room temperature before serving time to give the condensation time to evaporate.

For the garlic vinaigrette:

2 garlic cloves, minced

1 tablespoon Dijon mustard

$1/2$ cup extra virgin olive oil

$1/4$ cup white wine vinegar

Freshly ground black pepper and salt

For the salad:

1 pound yellow zucchini, sliced

1 pound yellow wax beans cut in 2-inch sections

1 medium yellow sweet pepper, chopped

1 pound green zucchini, sliced

1 pound green beans cut in 2-inch sections

4 tablespoons chopped scallion greens

$1/2$ teaspoon minced fresh savory

1 small red cabbage, shredded

1 medium red sweet pepper, chopped

3 red paste tomatoes, sliced

$1/3$ teaspoon red pepper flakes

1 medium orange sweet pepper, chopped

3 orange paste tomatoes, sliced

3 medium golden beets, steamed 30 minutes, peeled and sliced

For the honey vinaigrette:

$1/4$ cup extra virgin olive oil

1 teaspoon honey

2 tablespoons white wine vinegar

$1/8$ teaspoon red pepper flakes

To make the vinaigrettes: In two separate bowls, whisk together the ingredients for each of the vinaigrettes and set them aside.

To prepare the salad layers: Bring a large pot of salted water to a boil. First cook the yellow zucchini, then the yellow wax beans for 3 minutes each, or until just tender. After each batch is done, remove the vegetables from the cooking water with a slotted spoon and refresh them for a couple of seconds in a bowl of ice water to keep their color. Drain the vegetables and put them in a small bowl. Add the yellow pepper and toss with $1/4$ cup of garlic vinaigrette.

Repeat the process with the green zucchini and green beans. When the vegetables are at room temperature, toss the contents of the bowl with $1/4$ cup more of garlic vinaigrette. Set aside to marinate for about 10 minutes, then sprinkle with the scallions and savory.

Mix the shredded red cabbage with the remaning garlic vinaigrette and set it aside.

In a fourth bowl, combine the red pepper, red tomato, and red pepper flakes.

In a fifth bowl, combine the orange pepppers, the orange tomatoes, and the golden beets.

To assemble the salad: You will need a glass bowl 5 inches wide and 8 inches deep. A traditional footed trifle bowl works well. Each layer of vegetables needs to be about 1 inch thick.

Build the salad by first layering the marinated yellow vegetables 1 inch deep on the bottom. On top of this create a green layer. Create the third purple layer with the red cabbage.

Cover with the red layer and finally the orange layer. Glaze the top of the salad with the honey dressing. Serve immediately.

Serves 12 to 14 for a buffet.

Red, White, and Blue Potato Salad

This potato salad is an eye-catching addition to luncheons, particularly around the Fourth of July and elections. If you have no blue potatoes in your garden, they are occasionally available from specialty produce markets. Select only the deep blue-fleshed potatoes as the light and medium blue-fleshed ones turn an unappetizing gray when boiled. Blue-fleshed potatoes can be used in any potato salad recipe, but the color is best featured when a clear dressing is used.

For the dressing:

 2 tablespoons rich chicken stock
 1/4 cup white wine vinegar
 2 tablespoons dry white wine or
 white vermouth
 Salt and freshly ground pepper to
 taste
 1/2 cup extra virgin olive oil
 1 tablespoon chopped parsley
 1 tablespoon fresh chopped tarragon

For the salad:

 4 medium white boiling potatoes
 4 medium deep blue-fleshed potatoes (or 2 blue- and 2 red-
 fleshed potatoes)
 1/2 cup thinly sliced red bell
 peppers
 1/2 teaspoon freshly ground pepper

To make the dressing: In a small bowl, mix the chicken stock, vinegar, wine, salt, and pepper until the salt is dissolved. Slowly, whisk in the olive oil. Add the parsley and the tarragon and stir well to combine.

To make the salad: In two separate pots, boil the 2 or 3 colors of potatoes for 20 to 30 minutes until just barely tender when stuck with a fork. While still warm, peel the potatoes and slice them into 1/4-inch-thick slices.

Place the potatoes in a large salad bowl, alternating layers of blue and white potatoes with the red peppers. Pour the dressing over the still-warm potatoes and sprinkle with the pepper. Toss gently so the dressing gets evenly dispersed and the potatoes don't fall apart. (If the potatoes are overcooked or the mixing is too vigorous it will cause the separate colors of potatoes to mingle and the result will be a muddy looking salad.)

Let the salad sit for 3 or 4 hours so the flavors will meld. Serve the salad at room temperature or chilled.

Serves 4 to 6.

Multi-Colored Tomato Wedges

This salad is a simple but elegant way to show off the kaleidoscope of tomato colors in your garden.

For the vinaigrette:

 1 1/2 tablespoons balsamic vinegar
 1 teaspoon chopped fresh thyme
 leaves
 1/4 cup extra virgin olive oil
 Optional: salt and pepper

For the salad:

 3 red paste tomatoes
 2 orange gold paste tomatoes
 1 yellow tomato
 2 'Green Zebra' tomatoes
 1 purple tomato
 Garnish: sprigs of fresh thyme

To make the salad: In a small bowl, combine the vinaigrette ingredients and whisk until they emulsify. Set aside.

Cut the tomatoes into equal-sized wedges. Arrange them in a shallow round or oval bowl so the skin sides of the tomatoes are showing. Drizzle them with the vinaigrette and garnish with the fresh thyme sprigs.

Serves 6.

Braised Red Cabbage

This dish is most often associated with northern France and Germany. The brilliant red color is achieved by adding acidic vinegar and red wine to the cabbage. Serve this cabbage dish with roast chicken or pork and mashed potatoes.

2 tablespoons butter

1 onion, thinly sliced

1 medium red cabbage, shredded (about 8 cups)

1 tart apple, peeled, cored, and sliced

1 tablespoon sugar

1 tablespoon red wine vinegar

1/2 cup good red wine

1 bay leaf

Salt and freshly ground black pepper

Melt the butter in a Dutch oven or a soup pot. Add the onions and sauté them over medium heat until they are soft, about 7 minutes. Add the cabbage, apple, sugar, vinegar, red wine and the bay leaf. Stir the ingredients together and simmer on low for 30 to 40 minutes, or until the cabbage is tender. Remove the bay leaf and season with salt and pepper.

Serves 6.

Grilled Red and Gold Peppers with Melted Anchovies, Garlic, and Basil Sauce

This is one of Renee Shepherd's favorite recipes. Once I made it I had to agree. She developed it when working with her cooking partner Fran Raboff. Accompany the peppers with slices of crusty bread.

2 large sweet peppers, one red and one yellow

1 tablespoon extra virgin olive oil

1–2 ounce can anchovies, drained and coarsely chopped

6 garlic cloves, minced

2 tablespoons balsamic vinegar

1/2 cup chopped fresh Italian parsley

1/2 cup chopped fresh basil

Preheat a charcoal grill. Remove the seeds and membranes from the peppers and cut them lengthwise into 1-inch-wide strips. Brush them with olive oil and grill them over charcoal until they are slightly charred and tender, from 5 to 7 minutes. Put the peppers aside.

In a heavy skillet, heat one tablespoon of olive oil. Add the chopped anchovies and the garlic and cook over low to medium heat, stirring, until the anchovies melt and the garlic is fragrant, about 2 to 3 minutes. Stir in the balsamic vinegar. Add the parsley and basil and remove from the heat.

Arrange the grilled pepper strips on a serving platter and spoon the sauce over them. Serve immediately.

Serves 4.

Golden Tomato Tart

This spectacular tart can be served as an appetizer or as an entree for a light lunch. It is quite dramatic, made with gold tomatoes or any combination of colorful homegrown luscious tomatoes. Any leftover marinade can be used as a base for a vinaigrette dressing.

For the marinated tomatoes:

    4 to 5 medium gold tomatoes,
        thinly sliced
    6 to 7 gold cherry or pear toma-
        toes, halved
    $1/2$ cup extra virgin olive oil
    1 to 2 garlic cloves, crushed
    2 tablespoons chopped fresh
        parsley
    1 tablespoon minced fresh chives
    Freshly ground black pepper

For the filling:

    1 cup soft goat cheese or natural
        cream cheese
    3 to 4 tablespoons heavy cream
    1 tablespoon minced fresh
        rosemary
    1 9-inch prebaked pie shell

Put both kinds of tomatoes into a bowl. In another bowl combine the ingredients for the marinade. Set aside $1/4$ cup of the marinade and pour the rest over the sliced tomatoes. Marinate them for at least 1 hour.

In a mixing bowl, combine the cheese with the cream and work them into a smooth, creamy consistency that will spread easily. Mix in the rosemary and spread the cheese mixture over the cooled pie crust.

Arrange drained tomato slices in a single-layered circular pattern over cheese mixture, using the large slices for the outside and one slice for the middle. Fill in between the rows of large tomatoes with halved cherry tomatoes. Refrigerate until ready to serve. Just before serving, glaze the tomatoes with a $1/4$ cup of the marinating mixture.

Serves 6 as an appetizer.

Grandma Alice's Summer Vegetables

This recipe was given to me by Renee Shepherd of Renee's Garden. Renee's Grandma Alice made this dish for her when she was a kid after she let her pick all the vegetables. Renee loved all the colors. Here, the onions and carrots add sweetness while the fresh squash tastes quite nutty and creamy.

When I tried it I used small squash cut in pieces, as Renee recommends. Subsequently, I have also made it using only the tiniest baby squashes, such as pattypans, crooknecks, and zucchini, along with baby carrots. In that case, the squash and carrots should be left whole to really enjoy their beauty.

4 to 5 cups green and gold summer squashes, cut into 1-inch pieces (4 to 5 medium squashes)

1 cup sliced carrots (2 medium carrots)

1 large onion, coarsely chopped

1 cup rich chicken stock

2 tablespoons butter

2 1/2 tablespoons chopped fresh dill

1 tablespoon chopped fresh Italian parsley

Salt and freshly ground black pepper

2 tablespoons freshly grated Parmesan or Asiago cheese

In a 3-quart Dutch oven, combine the vegetables with the chicken broth and the butter. Bring the mixture to a boil and then reduce the heat and simmer for about 8 to 10 minutes or until the carrots and squash are just tender.

Remove the pan from the heat and mix in the dill, parsley, salt and pepper. Serve immediately with the freshly grated Parmesan or Asiago cheese.

Serves 6.

Show-Off Barbecued Vegetables

One of the tastiest and showiest ways to prepare summer vegetables is a quick and easy adaptation of the ever-popular barbecue. Although meat, fish, or poultry can be a nice complement, the vegetables are so good cooked this way; one is tempted to dispense with the rest.

If you are limited by the size of your grill you may have to cook the vegetables in more than one batch. Also consider that some of the vegetables cook at different rates. Peppers need the least amount of time, followed by the eggplant, squash, and onions.

For the seasoned oil:

- 1 cup extra virgin olive oil
- 2 garlic cloves, crushed
- 1/4 cup minced fresh basil or 1 tablespoon minced fresh rosemary

For the vegetables:

- 2 (medium to large) eggplants, cut into 1/2-inch-thick rounds
- 2 to 4 assorted colored summer squash, depending on their size (if large, cut diagonally into 1/2-inch-thick slices; if small, slice lengthwise into halves or leave whole)
- 4 small red onions whole, or 1 large onion, quartered
- 2 to 4 sweet red or yellow peppers, halved and seeded
- Salt and freshly ground black pepper

To make the seasoned oil: In a small bowl, mix the olive oil, garlic, and herbs and let them marinate at least 2 hours. (Refrigerate them if they are left to stand much longer).

To make the vegetables: Prepare the barbecue with charcoal and preheat. Meanwhile, place the vegetable slices on a cookie sheet and brush them with the seasoned oil. When the coals die down and are ready, spread them evenly around the bottom of the barbecue kettle. Place the vegetables oiled-side down on the grill. Brush the top sides of the vegetables with the oil and turn them when they are starting to brown.

Cooking time will vary in accordance with heat, distance from coals, and size and density of the vegetables. Over medium coals, expect average cooking time to be about 4 minutes on the first side and 3 minutes on the second side, but watch them carefully. Cook the vegetables until they are just tender, as they will fall apart if they are overcooked. Sprinkle with salt and pepper and serve.

Serves 4.

Cauliflower Mold with Lemon-Leek Béchamel Sauce

This is a fun way to feature differently colored cauliflower.

For the mold:

> 1 head each of yellow, white, and
> Romanesco cauliflower (about 1
> pound each)
> 1 teaspoon butter

To make the mold: Cut equal-sized florets off the cauliflower. In a large pot bring 3 cups of water to a rolling boil. First cook the white cauliflower for 4 minutes and then the yellow and Romanesco. Drain the florets and reserve about 1/2 cup of the cooking water.

Butter a rounded stainless steel or glass bowl (about 8 inches wide and 5 inches deep). Line the bowl with alternating cauliflower colors, starting with a cluster of Romanesco in the center, then a ring of white, then yellow, and so on, until the bowl is filled. All the florets should have their stems pointing inward and their florets pressed against the bowl.

Fill the center with smaller pieces and sprinkle with salt and pepper. Cover the mold with buttered parchment paper and press down lightly to compact.

For the sauce:

> 2 tablespoons butter
> 1 leek, light green parts only, sliced
> and cleaned (about 1 cup)
> 2 tablespoons all-purpose flour
> 1 cup milk
> 1/4 cup cooking water from the
> cauliflower

> 2 tablespoons fresh lemon juice
> Dash of freshly grated nutmeg
> Salt and freshly ground black pepper

To make the sauce: In a saucepan melt the butter and over medium heat sauté the leeks until tender, about 10 minutes. Add the flour and cook for another 2 minutes while stirring.

Add the milk a little at a time, continuing to stir until the sauce is free of lumps. Add 1/4 cup of the cauliflower cooking water, the lemon juice, a grating of nutmeg and the salt and pepper to taste. If the sauce is too thick, add a little more cooking water and reserve.

Before serving, reheat the mold in a hot water bath for 10 minutes. To serve, place a warm plate on top of the mold and invert the mold with the plate. Gently remove the mold. Serve with the lemon-leek béchamel sauce.

Serves 6.

Yellow Tomatoes Stuffed with Shrimp and Salsa

not as easy to hollow out without having them rip.

4 large yellow stuffing tomatoes

1 medium avocado

1 teaspoon fresh lemon juice

$1/2$ pound cooked baby shrimp

1 cup fresh salsa, or your favorite commercial salsa

Garnish: sprigs of fresh cilantro

This is quick, but zesty first course for a summer dinner. The unusual tomatoes will throw your guests for a loop. Stuffing tomatoes have an extra large cavity and fairly solid walls. Other large tomatoes can be used for this recipe but they are just

Cut the top off the stuffing tomatoes and remove the seeds and liquid from the cavity. Stand them upright on a serving plate. If they are not even on the bottom, carefully slice a little off the bottom to make them level, but be careful to not cut through the outside wall.

Cut the avocado into $1/2$-inch cubes, place in a bowl, sprinkle with the lemon juice and stir. Add the baby shrimp and the salsa and gently mix the ingredients together. Stuff the tomato cavities with the filling and garnish with the cilantro leaves.

Serves 4.

Sunny Delight Squash Blossom Omelet

Squash blossoms can be combined with red peppers and yellow zucchini for a colorful and especially tasty entrée. Choose from 'Sunny Delight', 'Gold Rush', 'Golden Dawn', 'Sunburst', and 'Yellow Crookneck' yellow summer squashes for the brightest colors.

For the filling:

2 tablespoons extra virgin olive oil

1 medium red onion, thinly sliced

1 garlic clove, minced

1 medium red bell pepper, seeded and chopped

6 baby yellow and green summer squash, cut in half lengthwise

6 large squash blossoms

2 tablespoons chopped fresh basil

1/2 teaspoon salt

Freshly ground black pepper

For the omelet:

1 teaspoon olive oil

6 large eggs

4 tablespoons grated Parmesan cheese

Garnish: 2 tablespoons snipped fresh chives and extra whole squash blossoms

To make the filling: In a large nonstick sauté pan, heat the olive oil and sauté the onions over medium heat until soft, about 7 minutes. Add the garlic and bell peppers and cook for 5 minutes or until tender. Remove the onion mixture to a bowl and set it aside. Put the yellow and green summer squash in the same pan and sauté them until lightly browned. Combine the onion mixture with the squash in the pan.

Carefully open the squash blossoms and remove any possible critters. Remove the stamens and pistils and coarsely chop the flowers. Add the chopped blossoms and the basil to the zucchini pan, season with the salt and pepper, cover and set aside.

To make the omelet: In a small mixing bowl, mix 3 of the eggs using a fork. In a nonstick 8- to 10-inch sauté pan, heat the olive oil until hot, but not smoking. Pour the eggs into the pan (they should sizzle). Tilt the pan in a few directions to assure that the mixture evenly coats the pan. Give the mixture a gentle shake to make sure it is not sticking. With a spatula, gently lift sections of the cooked portions and let a little of the uncooked egg flow underneath.

When most of the egg is set but the top is still moist, sprinkle 2 tablespoons of the Parmesan cheese over one half of the omelet. Spoon half of the vegetable filling over the cheese. With a spatula make sure the omelet is not sticking and then gently fold the other half of the omelet over the filling.

Slide the omelet onto a preheated plate, garnish with the chives and squash blossoms. Repeat the process for the second omelet.

Serves 2.

82

Rainbow Pepper Pizza with Pesto

Colorful wedges of peppers arranged in a color shift on a pesto base makes this pizza party fare. It can be made with only one or two colors of peppers and in any pattern, it will taste the same.

For the pesto:

- 2/3 cup extra virgin olive oil
- 4 tablespoons pine nuts
- 4 garlic cloves, minced
- 2 1/2 cups loosely packed fresh basil leaves
- 2/3 cup freshly grated Parmesan cheese
- Salt and freshly ground black pepper

For the pizza:

- 1 tablespoon extra virgin olive oil
- 1 large yellow onion, thinly sliced
- 1/4 teaspoon red pepper flakes, or to taste
- 1/2 cup fresh basil leaves, chopped
- 1/2 teaspoon dry oregano leaves
- 1 cup plus 1/2 cup grated mozzarella cheese (about 6 ounces)
- A combination of red, yellow, orange, ivory, and green bell peppers cut into thin strips with colors kept separate (about 1/3 cup of each color)
- 1 12-inch prebaked commercial pizza shell

To make the pesto: In a blender or food processor, place 3 tablespoons of the olive oil, the pine nuts, garlic, and the basil. Process for 1 minute or so, stopping the machine occasionally to push the basil leaves down and clean the sides of the container. Continue processing, adding the rest of the olive oil. Process until the mixture is smooth. Transfer the pesto to a bowl, stir in the Parmesan cheese and season to taste with salt and freshly ground black pepper.

To make the pizza: Preheat the oven to 450°F. Spread the pesto evenly up to 1 inch from the edge of the pizza shell.

In a large nonstick frying pan, heat the olive oil and sauté the onions over medium heat until translucent, about 7 minutes. Spread the onions evenly over the pesto base.

Sprinkle the pepper flakes, chopped basil, oregano, and 1 cup of mozzarella cheese evenly over the onion mixture.

Place the orange and red pepper slices in a single layer in the frying pan used for the onions and gently sauté until they are limp but not brown. Add a little oil if they start to stick. (To simplify the recipe, all the peppers can be cooked together. If you want to achieve a rainbow effect, however, you need to separate the red and orange peppers from each other and the other colors as their pigments bleed.)

Repeat the process, cooking the yellow, ivory, and green peppers together. To give the rainbow effect, keep the red peppers separate and arrange them over a fifth of the pizza in a wedge pattern. Repeat the process with the orange, yellow, ivory, and green bell peppers, covering the whole pizza shell in a wedge pattern. Sprinkle the remaining 1/2 cup mozzarella cheese evenly over the peppers.

Bake for 12 to 14 minutes, or until the cheese has melted and started to brown.

Serves 4.

Technicolor Nachos

Tortilla chips and peppers come in many colors. This recipe is a variation on a tried-and-true restaurant dish.

  12 ounces corn tortilla chips (red or
      blue or a combination of both)
  1 pound of pepper Jack cheese,
      grated
  1 1/2 cups roasted pepper strips, of
      all different colors
  1 teaspoon ground cumin
  2 tablespoon freshly chopped
      cilantro
  1 cup fresh salsa, or your favorite
      commercial salsa

Preheat the oven to 350°F. Place one layer of chips in a baking dish. Sprinkle with 1/3 each of the cheese, the pepper strips, and the cumin. Repeat with a second and third layer. Bake until the cheese has melted and started to brown, about 3 to 5 minutes. Watch carefully to avoid burning the chips. Garnish the nachos with the cilantro and serve with the salsa.

Serves 4.

Kaleidoscope Tacos

These unusually colorful tacos are best served "do-it-yourself" style. Every diner assembles their own, according to taste.

For the guacamole:

  1 ripe avocado
  1 teaspoon fresh lime juice
  1 teaspoon sour cream
  1/2 teaspoon chile powder

Cut the avocado in half; remove the pit and the peel. In a small bowl, mash the avocado with a fork, add the lime juice, sour cream, and chile powder. Mix until smooth and creamy. Place in a small bowl, cover with plastic wrap, and refrigerate until ready to serve.

For the salsa:

  2 yellow or orange tomatoes,
      chopped
  2 tablespoons chopped red onion
  1 small avocado, peeled, pitted,
      and chopped
  1 teaspoon minced jalapeño pepper
  1 tablespoon minced fresh cilantro
  2 tablespoons fresh lime juice
  2 tablespoons extra virgin olive oil
  1/4 teaspoon ground cumin
  1/8 teaspoon salt
  Freshly ground black pepper

In a bowl, combine the tomatoes, red onion, avocado, jalapeño pepper, and the cilantro with the lime juice, olive oil, cumin, and salt and pepper. Cover with plastic wrap and set aside.

For the taco filling:

  4 ears Ruby Queen corn, husked
  1 (15-ounce) can black beans
  1/2 pound French feta cheese,
      sliced
  1 yellow or orange bell pepper,
      sliced
  6 leaves romaine lettuce, chopped
  12 corn tortillas (1 14-ounce
      package)

Cook the ears of corn in the microwave on high for about 2 minutes each. (Cooking them in the microwave will preserve the red color.) With a sharp knife, cut off the kernels. Set them aside in a small bowl.

Drain the beans into a sieve; rinse them with cold water and set aside in a small bowl. Place cheese, peppers, and lettuce in separate bowls.

To make the tacos: Preheat the grill. Toast the corn tortillas on the hot grill for 10 to 20 seconds on each side. Present the guacamole, salsa, and the filling ingredients in bowls at the dining table.

Each diner should fill a tortilla with about 1 tablespoon each of guacamole, salsa, corn kernels, and the black beans, then add several slices of feta cheese, bell pepper, romaine, and then fold them together to eat.

Serves 4.

Mystery Marinara

This dish can really confuse guests. If you do not tell them it's made with tomatoes, they rarely guess correctly. The light-colored tomatoes are generally sweeter than the red ones and have an elusive taste of their own. Serve this meal with a salad and a crusty French baguette.

> 2 pounds white or cream-colored tomatoes: 'Locerno's Ivory Pearl', or 'White Beauty'
> 1 tablespoon butter
> 1 small onion, minced (about $^2/_3$ cup)
> 2 garlic cloves, minced

> $^1/_2$ teaspoon dried herbs: choose a combination of marjoram, thyme, rosemary, and oregano
> Salt and freshly ground black pepper
> 1 pound fresh spinach fettuccine
> $^1/_3$ cup heavy cream
> Grated Parmesan cheese

Put the tomatoes into a large saucepan and pierce their skins with a sharp knife. Cover and bring to the boil, then simmer for about 5 minutes, or until the tomatoes are soft. Transfer them to a food mill and strain out the seeds and skins (I use the food mill attachment to my stand mixer).

In a sauté pan, melt the butter and sauté the onions and garlic over low heat for about 7 minutes or until the onions are translucent.

Return the tomato puree to the saucepan and add the onion and garlic mixture and the herbs. Simmer the sauce over low heat till it has reduced to 1 $^1/_2$ cups, about 40 minutes. (Most light-colored tomatoes are quite juicy and need to be cooked quite a long time.) Season with salt and pepper to taste.

Meanwhile, cook the fettuccine according to the directions on the package. Drain and put them into a warm serving bowl. Add the cream to the sauce and stir. Heat the sauce to serving temperature, but do not boil or it will separate. Pour the sauce over the fettuccine and serve with grated Parmesan cheese.

Serves 4 to 6.

Golden Chard Dessert Tart

It is not unusual in Italy to have ricotta cheese in a tart. This version is enriched with golden grapes and chard. It makes a lovely, not-too-sweet finale to a meal.

For the crust:

- 2 cups all-purpose flour
- 1/2 cup ground blanched almonds
- 1/4 cup sugar
- 3/4 cup butter, cut in small pieces, at room temperature
- 1 egg yolk

For the filling:

- 3 eggs
- 15 ounces low-fat ricotta cheese
- 1/4 cup honey
- 1/4 cup dry white wine
- Dash of grated nutmeg
- 2 cups finely chopped golden chard leaves and tender stems, (about 5 medium leaves)
- 1 tablespoon chopped fresh mint
- 1 1/2 cups grated yellow squash, (about 1 large squash)

To make the crust: In the bowl of a stand mixer combine the flour, almonds, and sugar and stir. Add the butter and the egg yolk to the dry ingredients. Using the paddle attachment, beat on medium speed until the mixture is the texture of coarse corn meal. Gather into a ball, wrap in plastic wrap and refrigerate the dough for 15 minutes.

Preheat the oven to 375°F. Press the dough evenly into a 9-inch tart or pie pan. Cover it with parchment paper or aluminum foil and chill the crust for 15 minutes. Before prebaking the shell, fill its cavity with dry beans or rice to weigh down the crust so it will not bubble up. Bake for 10 minutes. Remove the paper and the beans and rice used as weights and reserve.

To prepare the filling: In a mixing bowl, blend the eggs with the cheese, honey, wine, and nutmeg. Then fold in the chard, mint, and squash. Pour the filling into the warm pie shell and bake it on the middle shelf of the oven for 50 minutes or until golden brown. The filling should be set when a toothpick inserted in the center comes out clean.

Serves 6 to 8.

Sunshine Zucchini Pancakes with Salsa

Most often, I serve these pancakes with salsa for a light supper; but for breakfast I omit the onions and serve them with maple syrup. This is a fun dish to make with children. If they want to do it all by themselves, a package of corn muffin mix works well. Follow the directions for corn-meal pancakes and add the vegetables to the wet mixture.

- 3/4 cup all-purpose flour, sifted
- 2 1/2 teaspoons baking powder
- 1 tablespoon sugar
- 1 1/4 cups yellow cornmeal
- 3/4 teaspoon salt
- 1 egg
- 1 cup milk
- 2 tablespoons vegetable oil
- 1 cup grated yellow summer squash or yellow zucchini, (about 1 1/2 medium)
- 3 tablespoons yellow bell pepper, seeded and chopped fine
- 3 tablespoons finely chopped onion
- 1 cup fresh salsa, or your favorite commercial salsa

In a medium bowl, put flour, baking powder, sugar, cornmeal and salt. Blend with a spoon. In another small bowl, put the egg, milk, oil, squash, pepper, and onion. Mix the wet ingredients with a spoon. Pour over the dry ingredients and stir lightly until just barely moist.

Heat a nonstick frying pan or griddle, then cook 2 or 3 pancakes at a time over medium heat until both sides are golden brown and the insides are firm. Keep the pancakes warm in a low oven until all are cooked. Serve the pancakes with the salsa.

Makes 8 to 10 3-inch pancakes.

True-Blue
Pancakes

These delicious, hearty pancakes get their lovely blue-green hue from the blue cornmeal and, of course, the blueberries.

  3/4 cup all-purpose flour, sifted

  2 1/2 teaspoons baking powder

  1 tablespoon sugar

  1 1/4 cups blue cornmeal

3/4 teaspoon salt

1 egg

1 cup milk

2 tablespoons vegetable oil

1 cup fresh blueberries

Garnish: more fresh blueberries

In a medium bowl, put the flour, baking powder, sugar, cornmeal, and salt. Blend with a spoon. In another small bowl, put the egg, milk, and oil. Mix the wet ingredients with a spoon and pour them over the dry ingredients and lightly stir until the batter is just barely moist. Fold in the blueberries.

Heat a frying pan or griddle, lightly grease it, then cook 2 or 3 pancakes at a time over medium heat until both sides are golden brown and the insides are firm. Keep the pancakes warm in a low oven until all are cooked.

Stack the pancakes and serve them with maple syrup and more fresh blueberries.

Makes 8 to 10 3-inch pancakes.

appendix A planting and maintenance

This section covers the basics of planning a vegetable garden, preparing the soil, starting seeds, transplanting, fertilizing, composting, using floating row covers, rotating crops, mulching, watering and installing irrigation, and maintaining vegetables.

Planning Your Vegetable Garden

Vegetables are versatile. You can interplant a few colorful varieties among your ornamentals—many vegetables grow well in the same conditions as annual flowers. Or you can add ribbons and accents of color to your existing vegetable garden. Or you can create an entire rainbow garden from rough sketch to harvest. In addition, most vegetables grow well in containers and large planter boxes.

The first step in planning any vegetable garden is choosing a suitable site. Most chefs recommend locating the edible garden as close to the kitchen as possible, and I heartily agree. Beyond that, the majority of vegetables need at least six hours of sun (eight is better)—except in warm, humid areas, where afternoon or some filtered shade is best—and good drainage.

Annual vegetables need fairly rich soil with lots of organic matter. Note the type of soil you have and how well it drains. Is it fertile and rich with organic matter? Is it so sandy that water drains too fast and few plants grow well? Or is there a hardpan under your garden that prevents roots from penetrating the soil or water from draining? Poor drainage is a fairly common problem in areas of heavy clay, especially in many parts of the Southwest with caliche soils—a very alkaline clay.

It's important to answer such basic questions before proceeding because annual vegetables should grow quickly and with little stress to be tender and mild. Their roots need air; if the soil stays waterlogged, roots suffocate or are prone to root rot. If you are unsure of the drainage in a particular area in your garden, dig a hole about 10 inches deep and 10 inches wide where you plan to put your garden. Fill the hole with water immediately and again the following day. If there's water in the whole eight to ten hours later, find another spot in the garden that will drain much faster. Amend the soil gen-erously with organic matter and mound it up at least 6 to 8 inches above the ground level. Or grow your vegetables in containers. Very sandy soil that drains too fast also calls for adding copious amounts of organic matter.

Find out the garden soil pH and nutrient levels with a soil test kit purchased from a local nursery or your state's university extension service, which can also lead you to sources of soil tests and soil experts. Most vegetables grow best in soil with a pH between 6.0 to 7.0—in other words, slightly acidic. Soil below 6.0 ties up phosphorus, potassium, and calcium, making them unavailable to plants; soil with a pH much higher than 6.5 ties up iron and zinc. As a rule, rainy climates have acidic soil that needs the pH raised, usually by adding lime; arid climates have fairly neutral or alkaline soil that needs extra organic matter to lower the pH.

After deciding where you are going to plant, it's time to choose your plants. See "Designing a Rainbow Garden" for suggested vegetables and flowers. Be sure to select species and varieties that grow well in your climate. As a rule, gardeners in northern climates and high elevations do well with vegetables that tolerate cool and/or short-summer conditions. Many vegetable varieties bred for short seasons and most salad greens are great for these conditions. Gardeners in hot, humid climes have success with plants that tolerate diseases well and are especially heat tolerant.

The USDA Plant Hardiness Zone Map has grouped eleven zones according to winter temperature lows, a help in choosing perennial plants but of limited use for annual vegetables. The new *Sunset National Garden Book,* published by Sunset Books, gives much more useful climatic information; it divides the continent into forty-five growing zones. Several regional maps describe the temperature ranges and growing season in detail. The maps are an integral part of this information-packed resource. Of additional interest to the vegetable gardener is the AHS Plant Heat-Zone Map, published by the American Horticultural Society. The heat map details twelve zones that indicate the average number of days each year when a given area experiences temperatures of 86°F or higher—the temperature at which many plants, including peas and most salad greens, begin to suffer physiological damage. In "The Rainbow Vegetable Encyclopedia" on page 21, I indicate which varieties have a low tolerance to high temperatures and those that grow well in hot weather. See the Bibliography for information on obtaining the heat map.

Other design considerations include bed size, paths, and fences. A garden of a few hundred square feet or more benefits from a path or two with the soil arranged in beds. Paths through any garden should be at least 3 feet wide to provide ample room for walking and using a wheelbarrow; beds should generally be limited to 5 feet across—the average distance a person can reach into the bed to harvest or pull weeds from both sides. Protection too is often needed, so consider putting a fence or wall around the garden to give it a stronger design and to keep out rabbits, woodchucks, and the resident dog. Assuming you have chosen a nice sunny area, selected a design, and determined that your soil drains properly, you are ready to prepare the soil.

Installing a Vegetable Garden

Preparing The Soil

To prepare the soil for a new vegetable garden, first remove large rocks and weeds. Dig out any perennial weeds, especially perennial grasses like Bermuda and quack grass. Sift the soil and closely examine each shovelful to remove every little piece of grass root or they will regrow with a vengeance. Taking up part of a lawn requires removing the sod. For a small area, this can be done with a flat spade. Removing large sections, though, warrants renting a sod cutter. Next, when the soil is not too wet, spade over the area.

Most vegetables are heavy feeders and few soils support them without supplements of lots of organic matter and nutrients. The big-three nutrients are nitrogen (N), phosphorus (P), and potassium (K)—the elements most frequently found in fertilizers. Calcium, magnesium, and sulfur are also important plant nutrients. Plants also need a range of trace minerals for healthy growth—among them iron, zinc, boron, copper, and manganese. A soil test will indicate what your soil needs. In general, most soils benefit from at least an application of an organic nitrogen fertilizer. While it's hard to say what your soil needs without a test, the following gives a rough idea of how much organic fertilizer to apply per 100 square feet of average soil: for nitrogen, apply blood meal at 2 pounds, or fish meal at 2 $\frac{1}{4}$ pounds; for phosphorus, apply 2 pounds bonemeal; for potassium, apply kelp meal according to the package, or in acidic soils 1 $\frac{1}{2}$ pounds of wood ashes. Kelp meal also supplies most trace minerals. In subsequent years, adding so many nutrients will not be needed if composting and mulching are practiced, especially if you rotate crops and use cover crops as green manure.

After the area has been spaded, cover it with 4 or 5 inches of compost, 1 or 2 inches of well-aged manure, and any other needed fertilizers or lime. Shovel on a few more inches of compost if you live in a hot, humid climate where heat burns the compost at an accelerated rate, or if the soil is very alkaline, very sandy, or very heavy clay. Add lime at this point if the soil test indicates the garden soil is too acidic. Follow the directions on the package. Sprinkle fertilizers over the soil. Incorporate all the ingredients thoroughly by turning the soil with a spade and working the amendments into the top 8 to 12 inches. If your garden is large or the soil is very hard to work, consider using a rototiller. (When you put in a garden for the first time, a rototiller can be very helpful. However, research has shown that continued tiller use is hard on soil structure and quickly burns up valuable organic matter if used regularly.)

Finally, grade and rake the area. You are now ready to form the beds and paths. With all the added materials, the beds will be elevated above the paths—which further helps drainage. Slope the sides of the beds so that loose soil will not be easily washed or knocked onto the paths. Some gardeners add a brick or wood edging to outline the beds. Putting some sort of gravel, brick, stone, or mulch on the paths will forestall weed growth and prevent your feet from getting wet and muddy.

Before planting the garden, the last task is to provide support for vining crops like pole beans and tomatoes. There are many types of supports—from simple stakes to elaborate wire cages; whatever you choose, it's best to install them before you plant.

Starting from Seeds

You can grow all annual vegetables from seeds. They can be started indoors in flats or other well-drained containers, outdoors in a cold frame, or, depending on the time of year, directly in the garden. When I start annual vegetables inside, I seed them in either plastic pony packs recycled from the nursery or in Styrofoam compartmentalized containers variously called plugs or seedling trays (available from mail-order garden-supply houses). Whatever type of container you use, the soil depth should be 2 to 3 inches deep. A shallower container dries out too fast; deeper soil is usually a waste of seed-starting soil and water.

Starting seeds inside gives seedlings a safe place away from slugs and birds. It also allows gardeners in cold or hot climates to get a jump on the season. Many vegetables can be started four to six weeks before the last expected frost date, then transplanted into the garden as soon as the soil is workable. Furthermore, some vegetables are sensitive to high temperatures. By starting fall crops inside in mid- or late summer, the seeds will germinate and the seedlings will get a good start and be ready for transplant outside in early fall when the weather has started to cool.

The cultural needs of seeds vary widely among species. Still, some basic rules apply to most seeding procedures. First, whether starting seeds in the ground or in a container, use loose, water-retentive soil that drains well. Good drainage is important because seeds can get waterlogged, and too much water can lead to "damping off," a fungal disease that kills seedlings at the soil line. Commercial starting mixes are usually excellent as they have been sterilized to remove weed seeds; however, the quality varies greatly from brand to brand. I find most commercial mixes lack enough nitrogen, so I water with a weak solution of fish emulsion when planting the seeds, and again a week or so later.

Smooth the soil surface and plant the seeds at the recommended depth. Information on seed depth is included in "The Rainbow Vegetable Encyclopedia" on page 21, as well as on the back of most seed packages. Pat the seeds gently into the soil and water carefully to make the seed bed moist but not soggy. Mark the name of the plant, the variety, and the date of seeding on a plastic or wooden label; place the label at the head of the row.

If you are starting seeds in containers, put the seedling tray in a warm, but not hot, location to help seeds germinate more quickly.

When starting seeds outside, protect the seed bed with either floating row covers or bird netting to keep out critters. If slugs and snails are a problem, encircle the area with hardwood ashes or diatomaceous earth to repel them and go out at night with a flashlight to catch any that cross the barrier.

For seeds started inside, it's imperative that they have a quality source of light immediately after they have germinated;

otherwise, new seedlings will grow spindly and pale. A greenhouse, sun porch, and south-facing window with no overhang will suffice, provided the growing spot is warm. If bright ambient light is not available, use fluorescent lights, which are available from home-supply stores and specialty mail-order houses. Hang the lights just above the plants for maximum light (no farther than 3 or 4 inches away). Adjust the lights upward as the plants get taller. An alternative: If the temperature is above 60°F, I put my seedling trays outside on a table in the sun and protect them with bird netting during the day, then bring them in at night.

When seedlings have sprouted, keep them moist. If you have seeded thickly or have crowded plants, thin some. Using small scissors, cut the extra plants off, leaving the remaining seedlings an inch or so apart.

Do not transplant seedlings until they have their second set of true leaves. The first leaves that sprout from a seed are called seed leaves; they usually look different from the later-forming true leaves. If the seedlings are tender, wait until all danger of frost is past before setting them out. In fact, don't put heat-loving tomatoes and peppers out until the weather has thoroughly warmed up and stayed that way. Young plants started indoors should be "hardened off" before they are planted in the garden—that is, they should be put outside in a sheltered place for a few days in their containers to let them get used to the differences in external temperature, humidity, and air movement. A cold frame is perfect for hardening off plants.

Transplanting

I generally start annual vegetables from seeds, then transplant them outside. Occasionally I buy transplants from local nurseries. Before setting out transplants in the garden, I check to see if a mat of roots has formed at the bottom of the root ball. If so, I remove it or open it up so the roots won't continue to grow in a tangled mass. I set the plant in the ground at the same height as it was in the container, pat the plant in place gently by hand, and water each plant well to remove air bubbles. I space plants so that they won't be crowded once they've matured; when vegetables grow too close together, they're prone to rot diseases and mildew. If I'm planting on a very hot day or the transplants have been in

a protected greenhouse, I shade them with a shingle placed on the sunny side of the plants. Then I install my irrigation ooze tubing and mulch with a few inches of organic material. (See "Watering and Irrigation Systems" on page 95 for more information.) I keep the transplants moist but not soggy for the first few weeks.

Floating Row Covers

Among the most valuable tools for plant protection are floating row covers made of lightweight spunbond polyester or polypropylene fabric. Unfortunately, they are not particularly attractive, so they may be of limited use in a decorative rainbow garden. Laid directly over the plants, they "float" in place and protect plants against cold weather and pests.

If used correctly, row covers are a most effective pest control for cucumber, asparagus, bean, and potato beetles; squash bugs and vine borers; cabbage worms; leafhoppers; onion maggots; aphids; and leaf miners. The most lightweight covers, usually called summer-weight or insect barriers because they have little heat buildup, are useful for insect control throughout the season in all but the hottest climates. They reduce sunlight about 10 percent, which is seldom a problem unless your garden is shady. Heavier versions, sometimes called garden covers under trade names like Reemay, and Tufbell, variously block from 15 percent to 50 percent of the sunlight and guard against pests. They also raise the temperature underneath from 2°F to 7°F, which is usually enough to protect early and late crops from frost or to add warmth for heat-loving crops in cool-summer areas.

Besides effectively protecting plants from cold weather and many pests, floating row covers have numerous other advantages:

• The stronger ones protect plants from most songbirds, though not from crafty squirrels and blue jays.

• They raise the humidity around plants, a bonus in arid climates, but a problem with some crops in humid climates.

• They protect young seedlings from sunburn in summer and in high-altitude gardens.

There are a few limitations to consider:

• These covers keep out pollinating bees

and must be removed when squash, melons, and cucumbers are in production.

• They are not attractive enough to use over most flower beds and in decorative settings. In fact, they make the garden look like a sorority slumber party.

• Many of the fabrics last only a year before starting to deteriorate (I use tattered small pieces to cover containers and in the bottoms of containers to keep out slugs, etc.).

• Row covers are made from petroleum products and eventually end up in the landfill.

• In very windy areas, the tunnels and floating row covers are apt to be blown away or shredded.

• The heavyweight versions reduce sunlight considerably and are useful only to help raise temperatures when frost threatens.

Rolls of the fabric, from 5 to 10 feet wide and up to 100 feet long, can be purchased from local nurseries or ordered from garden-supply catalogs. As a rule, mail-order sources have a wider selection of materials and sizes.

Before applying your row cover, fully prepare the bed and make sure it's free of eggs, larvae, and adult pests. (For example, if instead of rotating your crops, you follow onions with onions in the same bed, you are apt to have larvae of the onion root maggot trapped under the cover with their favorite food and safe from predators!)

Then install drip irrigation if you are using it, plant your crop, and mulch (if appropriate). There are two ways to lay a row cover: either directly on the plants or stretched over wire hoops. Laying the cover directly on the plants is the easiest to install. However, laying it over hoops has the advantage of being easier to check underneath. Also, some plants are sensitive to abrasion when the wind whips the cover around, causing the plant tips to turn brown. When placing the cover directly on the plants, leave some slack so plants have room to grow. For both methods, secure the edges completely with bricks, rocks, old pieces of lumber, bent wire hangers, or U-shaped metal pins sold for this purpose.

To avoid unwanted surprises, it's critical to look under the row covers from time to time. Check soil moisture; the fibers sometimes shed rain and overhead irrigation

water. Check as well for weeds; the protective fiber aids their growth too. And most importantly, check for any insect pests that may be trapped inside.

Maintaining the Vegetable Garden

The backbone of appropriate maintenance is knowledge of your soil and weather, an ability to recognize basic water- and nutrient-deficiency symptoms, and a familiarity with the plants you grow.

Annual vegetables are growing machines. As a rule, they need to grow rapidly with few interruptions so they produce well and have few pest problems. Once the plants are in the ground, continually monitoring for nutrient deficiencies, drought, and pests can head off problems. Keep the beds weeded because weeds compete for moisture and nutrients. In normal soil, most vegetables benefit from supplemental nitrogen fertilizer. Fish emulsion and fish meal, blood meal, and chicken manure all have their virtues. Sandy or problem soils may require more nutrients to provide potassium and trace minerals. If so, apply kelp meal or kelp emulsion as well as the nitrogen sources mentioned above or add a packaged, balanced, organic vegetable fertilizer. For more specific information on fertilizing, see the individual entries in "The Rainbow Vegetable Encyclopedia" on page 21.

Weeding

Weeding is necessary to make sure unwanted plants don't compete with and overpower your vegetables. A good small triangular hoe will help you weed a small garden if the weeds are young, few, and easily hoed. When the weeds get large or out of control, you'll have to dedicate your muscles to a session of hand pulling. Applying a mulch is a great way to cut down on weeds; however, if there's a big problem with slugs in your garden, the mulch gives them more places to hide. Another means of controlling weeds, especially annual weeds like crabgrass and pigweed, is a new organic preemergence herbicide made from corn gluten called Concern Weed Prevention Plus. This gluten meal inhibits the tiny feeder roots of germinating weed seeds, so they wither and die. It does not kill existing weeds. Obviously, if you use it among new seedlings or in seed beds, it

kills them too, so it is only useful in areas away from very young plants.

Mulching

Mulching can save the gardener time, effort, and water. A mulch layer reduces moisture loss, prevents erosion, controls weeds, minimizes soil compaction, and moderates soil temperature. When the mulch is an organic material, it adds nutrients and organic matter to the soil as it decomposes, making heavy clay more porous, and helping sandy soil retain moisture. Mulches are often attractive additions to the garden. Applying a few inches of organic matter every spring helps keep most vegetable gardens healthy. Mulch with compost from your compost pile, pine needles, composted sawdust, straw, or one of the many agricultural byproducts like rice hulls or apple or grape pomace.

Black plastic mulch

Composting

Compost is the humus-rich result of the decomposition of organic matter such as leaves and garden trimmings. The objective of maintaining a composting system is to speed up decomposition and centralize the material so you can gather it up and spread it where it will do the most good. Compost is useful as a soil additive or a mulch. Compost's benefits include providing nutrients to plants in a slow-release, balanced fashion; helping break up clay soil; aiding sandy soil to retain moisture; and correcting pH problems. On top of that, compost is free! It can be made at home and is an excellent way to recycle our yard and kitchen "wastes."

There need be no great mystique about composting. To create the environment where decay-promoting microorganisms do all the work, just include the following four ingredients, mixed well: three or four parts

A three-bin composting system

"brown" material high in carbon, such as dry leaves, dry grass, or even shredded black-and-white newspaper; one part "green" material high in nitrogen, such as fresh grass clippings, fresh garden trimmings, barnyard manure, or kitchen trimmings like pea pods and carrot tops; water in moderate amounts so the mixture is moist but not soggy; and air to supply oxygen to the microorganisms. Bury the kitchen trimmings within the pile, so as not to attract flies. Cut up any large pieces of material. Exclude weeds that have gone to seed and noxious perennial weeds such as Bermuda grass because they can carry those weeds into your garden. Do not add meat, fat, diseased plants, woody branches, or cat or dog excrement.

I don't get stressed about the proper proportions of compost materials, as long as there's a fairly good mix of materials from the garden. If the decomposition is too slow, that's usually because the pile has too much brown material, is too dry, or needs air. If the pile smells, either it is too wet or contains too much green material. To speed up decomposition, I often chop or shred the materials before adding them to the pile. I may turn the pile occasionally to encourage additional oxygen throughout. During decomposition, the materials can become quite hot and steamy, which is great; however, it is not mandatory that the compost become extremely hot.

You can make compost in a simple pile, in wire or wood bins, or in rather expensive containers. The size should be about 3 feet high, wide, and tall for the most efficient decomposition and so the pile is easily workable. It can be up to 5 feet by 5 feet, but that's harder to manage. In a rainy climate it's a good idea to have a cover for the compost. I like to use three bins. I collect the compost materials in one bin; the second is a working bin; when the working bin is full, I turn its contents into the last bin for final decomposition. I sift the finished compost into empty garbage cans so the nutrients don't leach into the soil. Then the empty bin is ready to fill up again.

Crop Rotation

Crop rotation in the edible garden has been practiced for centuries for two reasons: to help prevent diseases and pests and to prevent depletion of nutrients from the soil, as some crops add nutrients and others remove them.

To rotate crops, you must know what plants are in which families as plants in the same families often are prone to the same diseases and pests and deplete the same nutrients.

The following is a short list of related vegetables:

Goosefoot family (Chenopodiaceae)—includes beets, chard, orach, spinach

Cucumber family (gourd) (Cucurbitaceae)—includes cucumbers, gourds, melons, summer squash, winter squash, pumpkins

Lily family (onion) (Liliaceae)—includes asparagus, chives, garlic, leeks, onions, Oriental chives, shallots

Mint family (Lamiaceae)—includes basil, mints, oregano, rosemary, sages, summer savory, thymes

Mustard family (cabbage) (Brassicaceae)—includes arugula, broccoli, cabbages, cauliflower, collards, cresses, kale, kohlrabi, komatsuna, mizuna, mustards, radishes, turnips

Nightshade family (Solanaceae)—includes eggplants, peppers, potatoes, tomatillos, tomatoes

Parsley family (carrot) (Apiaceae)—includes carrots, celeriac, celery, chervil, coriander (cilantro), dill, fennel, lovage, parsley, parsnips

Pea family (legumes) (Fabaceae)—includes beans, cowpeas, fava beans, lima beans, peanuts, peas, runner beans, soybeans, sugar peas

Sunflower family (composites) (Asteraceae)—includes artichokes, calendulas, celtuce, chicories, dandelions, endives, lettuces, marigolds, tarragon

The object to rotating crops is to avoid growing members of the same family in the same spot year after year. For example: cabbage, a member of the mustard family, should not be followed by radishes, a member of the same family, as both are prone to flea beetles and the flea beetle's eggs will be in the soil ready to hatch and attack the radishes. Tomatoes should not follow eggplants, as they are both prone to fusarium wilt.

Crop rotation is also practiced to help keep the soil healthy. One family, namely the pea family (legumes), that includes not only peas and beans but also clovers and alfalfa, adds nitrogen to the soil. In contrast, most members of the mustard (cabbage) family deplete the soil of nitrogen. Members of the nightshade and cucumber families are other heavy feeders. Because most vegetables deplete the soil, knowledgeable gardeners not only rotate their beds with vegetables from different families, they also include an occasional cover crop of clover or alfalfa and other soil benefactors like buckwheat and vetch to add what's called "green manure." The gardener allows these crops to grow for a few months, then turns them into or under the soil. As they decompose, they provide extra organic matter and many nutrients, help stop the pest cycle, and attract beneficial insects. Some cover crops (like rye) are grown over the winter to control soil erosion. The seeds of all sorts of cover crops are available from farm suppliers and specialty seed companies. I've been able to give only the basics on this subject; for more information, see Shepherd Ogden's *Step by Step Organic Vegetable Gardening* and some of the other basic gardening texts recommended in the Bibliography.

Watering and Irrigation Systems

Even gardeners who live in rainy climates may have to do supplemental watering at specific times during the growing season. Therefore, most gardeners need some sort of supplemental watering system and a knowledge of water management.

There is no easy formula for determining the correct amount or frequency of watering. Proper watering takes experience and observation. In addition to the specific watering needs of individual plants, watering requirements depends on soil type, wind conditions, and air temperature. To water properly, it's important to learn how to recognize water-stress symptoms (often a dulling of foliage color as well as the better-known symptoms of drooping leaves and wilting), how much to water (too much is as bad as too little), and how to water. Some general rules are:

1. Water deeply. Except for seed beds, most plants need infrequent, deep watering rather than frequent, light sprinkling.

2. To ensure proper absorption, apply water at a rate slow enough to soak deeply into the soil rather than run off.

3. Do not use overhead watering systems when the wind is blowing.

4. Try to water early in the morning so foliage has time to dry before nightfall, thus preventing some disease problems. In addition, less water evaporates in cooler temperatures.

5. Test your watering system occasionally to make sure it covers the area evenly.

6. Use methods and tools that conserve water. The pistol-grip nozzle on a hose will shut off the water while you move from one container or planting bed to another. Soaker hoses, made from either canvas or recycled tires, and other ooze- and drip-irrigation systems apply water slowly and more efficiently than overhead systems.

Drip, or the related ooze/trickle, irrigation systems are advisable wherever feasible; most gardens are well-suited to them. Drip systems deliver water a drop at a time through spaghetti-like emitter tubes or plastic pipe with emitters that drip water right onto the root zone of each plant. Because of the time and effort involved in installing one or two emitters per plant, these systems work best for permanent plantings such as in rose beds, with rows of daylilies and lavender say, or with trees and shrubs. Drip lines require continual maintenance to ensure the individual emitters are not clogged.

Similar systems, called ooze systems, deliver water through either holes made every 6 or 12 inches along solid flexible tubing or ooze along the entire porous hose. Neither system is as prone to clogging as are emitters. The solid type is made of plastic and is often called laser tubing. It is pressure-compensated, which means the water flow is even throughout the length of the tubing. The high-quality brands have a built-in mechanism to minimize clogging and are made of tubing that will not expand in hot weather and, consequently, pop off its fittings. (Some of the inexpensive drip-irrigation kits can make you crazy!) The porous hose types, made from recycled tires, come in two sizes—a standard hose diameter of 1 inch, great for shrubs and trees planted in a row, and $1/4$-inch tubing that's easy to snake around beds of small plants. Neither is pressure-compensated so the plants nearest the water source receive more water than those at the end of the line. It also means they will not work well if there is any slope. All types of drip emitter and ooze systems are installed after the plants

Baby lettuces with laser tubing drip irrigation

are in the ground and are held in place with ground staples. To use any drip or ooze system, it's also necessary to install an anti-siphon valve at the water source to prevent dirty garden water from being drawn into the house's drinking water and to include a filter to prevent debris from clogging the emitters.

To set up the system, connect 1-inch distribution tubing to the water source then arrange the tubing around the garden perimeter. Connect smaller-diameter drip and ooze lines to this. As you see, installing these systems requires some thought and time. You can order these systems from either a specialty mail-order garden or irrigation source or visit your local plumbing store. I find the latter to be the best solution for all my irrigation problems. Over the years, I've found that plumbing-supply stores offer professional-quality supplies, usually for less money than the so-called inexpensive kits available in home-supply stores and some nurseries. Their professionals also may help you work out an irrigation design tailored to your garden. Whether choosing an emitter or an ooze system or buying tubing, be prepared by bringing a rough drawing of the area to be irrigated—including dimensions, location of the water source, any slopes, and, if possible, the water pressure at the water source. Let the professionals walk you through the steps and help you pick out supplies to best fit your site.

Problems aside, all forms of drip irrigation are more efficient than furrow or standard overhead watering. They deliver water to its precise destination and are well worth considering. They provide water slowly, so it doesn't run off; they also water deeply, which encourages deep rooting. Drip irrigation also eliminates many disease problems, and there are fewer weeds because so little soil surface is moist. Finally, drip-irrigation systems have the potential to waste a lot less water.

appendix B
pest and disease control

The following sections cover a large number of pests and diseases. An individual gardener, however, will encounter few such problems in a lifetime of gardening. Good garden planning, good hygiene, and an awareness of major symptoms will keep problems to a minimum and give you many hours to enjoy your garden and feast on its bounty.

There are some spoilers, though, that sometimes need control. For years, controls were presented as a list of critters and diseases, followed by the newest and best chemicals to control them. Times have changed. We now know that chasing the latest chemical to fortify our arsenal is a bit like chasing our tail. That's because most pesticides, both insecticides and fungicides, kill beneficial insects as well as the pests; therefore, the more we spray, the more we are forced to spray. Nowadays, we know that successful pest control focuses on prevention, plus beefing up the natural ecosystem so beneficial insects are on pest patrol. How does that translate to pest control for the vegetable garden directly?

1. When possible, find and plant resistant varieties. For example, in cold, wet weather choose lettuce varieties resistant to downy mildew; if fungal diseases are a problem in your garden, select disease-resistant varieties of tomatoes.

2. Use mechanical means to prevent insect pests from damaging plants. For example, cover young squash and potato plants with floating row covers to protect them from squash borers and flea beetles; sprinkle wood ashes around plants to prevent cabbage root maggots and slug damage; and put cardboard collars around young tomato, pepper, cabbage, and squash seedlings to prevent cutworms from destroying them.

3. Clean up diseased foliage and dispose of it in the garbage to cut down on the cycle of infection.

4. Rotate your crops so that plants from the same family are not planted in the same place for two consecutive seasons.

5. Encourage and provide food for beneficial insects. In the vegetable garden, this translates into letting a few selected vegetables go to flower as well as growing flowering herbs and ornamentals to provide a season-long source of nectar and pollen for beneficial insects.

Beneficial Insects

In a nutshell, few insects are potential problems; most are either neutral or beneficial to the garden. Given the chance, the beneficials will do much of the insect control for you, provided that you don't use pesticides. Pesticides are apt to kill the beneficial insects as well as the problematic insects. Like predatory lions stalking zebra, predatory ladybugs (lady beetles) and lacewing larvae hunt and eat aphids that might be attracted to your lettuce, say. A miniwasp parasitoid will lay eggs on, or inside, those aphids. Spraying aphids, even with a so-called benign pesticide such as insecticidal soap or pyrethrum, will kill the ladybugs, lacewings, and that baby parasitoid wasp too.

Most insecticides are broad-spectrum, which means that they kill insects indiscriminately. In my opinion, organic gardeners who regularly use organic, broad-spectrum insecticides have missed this point. While they are technically using an "organic" pesticide, they actually may be eliminating the beneficial insects—a truly organic means of control.

Unfortunately, many gardeners are not only unaware of the benefits of the predator-prey relationship, they often are not able to recognize beneficial insects. The following sections will help you identify both the beneficial insects as well as the pest organisms. A hand lens is an invaluable, inexpensive tool that will also help you identify the insects in your garden. For a more detailed aid to identifying insects, see *Rodale's Color Handbook of Garden Insects* by Anna Carr.

Predators and Parasitoids

Insects that feed on other insects are divided into two types: the predators and the parasitoids. Predators are mobile. They stalk plants looking for such plant feeders as aphids and mites. Parasitoids, on the other hand, are insects that develop in or on the bodies, pupae, or eggs of other host insects. Most parasitoids are minute-sized wasps or flies whose larvae (young, immature stages of the insect) eat other insects from within. Some of the wasps are so small, they can develop inside an aphid or an insect egg. In other cases, one parasitoid egg can divide into several identical cells, each developing into identical miniwasp larvae that then can kill an entire caterpillar. Though nearly invisible to most gardeners, parasitoids are the most specific and effective means of insect control.

The predator-prey relationship can be a fairly stable situation. When the natural system is working properly, pest insects can inhabit the garden along with the predators and parasitoids without a problem.

Sometimes, though, the system breaks down. For example, a number of imported pests have taken hold in this country. Unfortunately, when such organisms were brought here, their natural predators did not accompany them. Four pesky examples are the Japanese beetle, the European brown snail, the white cabbage butterfly, and the flea beetle. None of these pests has natural enemies in the United States to provide balanced, sufficient controls. Where those imported pests occur, it is sometimes necessary to use physical means or selective pesticides that kill only the problem insect.

Weather extremes sometime produce imbalances as well. For example, long stretches of hot, dry weather favor grasshoppers that invade vegetable gardens, because the diseases that keep them in check are more prevalent under moist conditions. Predator-prey relationships also become imbalanced because common gardening practices often inadvertently work in favor of the pests. For example, when gardeners spray regularly with broad-spectrum pesticides, not all the garden insects are killed. As pests generally reproduce more quickly than predators and parasitoids, regular spraying usually tips the balance in favor of those pests. Further, the average yard full of grass and shrubs usually has few plants that produce nectar for beneficial insects. Adding a few squash plants and a row of lettuces for good measure won't help; the new, luscious growth will attract aphids but not the beneficials. Knowing the importance of ecological balance as well as safe and effective insect-control practices will help create a vegetable garden that is relatively free of many pest problems.

Attracting Beneficial Insects

Another key to promoting a healthy balance in your garden is providing a diversity of plants, including plenty of nectar- and pollen-producing varieties. Nectar is the primary food of many beneficial insects—adults and some larvae. Interplanting vegetables with flowers and numerous herbs helps attract beneficials. Ornamentals—like species zinnias, marigolds, alyssum, and yarrow—provide many flowers over a long season that are shallow enough for insects to reach the nectar. Large, dense flowers like tea roses and dahlias are nearly useless as their nectar is usually out of reach. Herbs rich in nectar include fennel, dill, anise, chervil, oregano, thyme, and parsley. Allowing a few vegetables like broccoli, carrots, and kale, in particular, to go to flower helps because their tiny flowers—full of nectar and pollen—are just what many beneficial insects like.

Following are a few of the predatory and parasitoid insects helpful in the garden. Their preservation and protection should be a major goal of your pest-control strategy.

Ground beetles and their larvae are all predators. Most adult ground beetles are fairly large black beetles that scurry out from under plants or containers when you disturb them. Their favorite foods are soft-bodied larvae like Colorado potato beetle larvae and root maggots (Root maggots eat cabbage-family plants.); some ground beetles even eat snails and slugs. If supplied with an undisturbed place to live, like a compost area or groupings of perennial plantings, ground beetles will be long-lived residents of your garden.

Lacewings are one of the most effective insect predators in the home garden. They are small green or brown gossamer-winged insects that in their adult stage eat flower nectar, pollen, aphid honeydew, and sometimes aphids and mealybugs. In the larval stage, they look like tiny tan alligators. Called aphid lions, lacewing larvae are fierce predators of aphids, mites, and whiteflies—all occasional pests that suck plant sap. If you have problems with sucking insects in your garden, consider purchasing lacewing eggs or larvae by mail-order to jump-start your lacewing population. Remember to plant lots of nectar plants so the population continues from year to year.

Lady beetles (ladybugs) are the best known of the beneficial garden insects. Actually, there are about four hundred species of lady beetles in North America alone. They come in a variety of colors and markings in addition to the familiar red with black spots, but lady beetles are never green. Lady beetles and their fierce-looking alligator-shaped larvae eat copious amounts of aphids and other small insects.

Spiders are close relatives of insects. There are hundreds of species. They are some of the most effective predators of a wide range of pest insects.

Syrphid flies (also called flower flies or hover flies) look like small bees hovering over flowers, but they have only two wings. Most have yellow and black stripes. Their larvae are small green maggots that inhabit leaves and eat small sucking insects and mites.

Wasps comprise a large family of insects with transparent wings. Unfortunately, the few large wasps that sting have given the family a bad name. In fact, all wasps are either insect predators or parasitoids. The miniwasps are usually parasitoids: the adult female lays her eggs in such insects as aphids, whitefly larvae, and caterpillars; the developing wasp larvae devour their host. These miniature wasps, available for purchase from insectaries, are especially effective when released in greenhouses.

Pests

The following pests are sometimes problems in the vegetable garden.

Aphids are soft-bodied, small, green, black, pink, or gray insects that produce many generations in one season. They suck plant juices and exude honeydew.

Sometimes, leaves under the aphids turn black from a secondary mold growing on the nutrient-rich honeydew. Aphids are primarily a problem on cabbages, broccoli, beans, lettuces, peas, and tomatoes. Aphid populations can escalate especially in the spring before beneficial insects are present in large numbers and when plants are covered by row covers or are growing in cold frames. The presence of aphids sometimes indicates that a plant is under stress. Is the cabbage getting enough water or sunlight? Check first to see if stress is a problem and then try to correct the situation. Also look for aphid mummies and other natural enemies mentioned above. Mummies are swollen, brown or metallic-looking aphids; a wasp parasitoid grows inside the mummy. They are valuable, so keep them.

Generally, to remove aphids wash the foliage with a strong blast of water; cut back the foliage if aphids persist. Fertilize and water the plant, then check on it in a few days. Repeat with the water spray a few more times. In extreme situations, spray with insecticidal soap or a neem product.

A number of **beetles** are garden pests. They include asparagus beetles, Mexican bean beetles, different species of cucumber beetles, flea beetles, and wireworms (the larvae of click beetles). All are problems throughout most of North America. Asparagus beetles look like elongated, red lady beetles with a black-and-cream-colored cross on their backs; they feed on asparagus.

Colorado potato beetles and Japanese beetles are primarily problems in the eastern United States. Mexican bean beetles look like brown lady beetles with oval black spots. As their name implies, they feed on beans. Cucumber beetles are ladybug-like green or yellow-green beetles with either black stripes or black spots. Their larvae feed on the roots of corn and other vegetables. The adults devour members of the cucumber family, corn tassels, beans, and some salad greens. Flea beetles are minuscule, black-and-white-striped beetles hardly large enough to be seen. Flea beetle grubs feed on the roots and lower leaves of many vegetables; the adults chew on the leaves of tomatoes, potatoes, eggplants, radishes, peppers, and other plants—causing the leaves to look shot full of tiny holes. The adult click beetle is rarely seen; its young, brown, 1 1/2-inch-long, shiny larva called a wire-

worm works underground—damaging tubers, seeds, and roots. Colorado potato beetles are larger and rounder than lady beetles; they have red-brown heads and black-and-yellow-striped backs. Primarily a problem in the eastern United States, they skeletonize the leaves of potatoes, tomatoes, eggplants, and peppers. Japanese beetles, mostly problematic east of the Mississippi, are fairly large, metallic blue or green beetles with coppery wings. The larval stage (a grub) eats the roots of grasses; the adult chews its way through beans, asparagus plants, and many ornamentals.

The larger beetles, if not found in great numbers, can be controlled by hand-picking. Morning picking is best, when the beetles move slower. Knock them into a bowl of soapy water. Flea beetles are too small to gather by hand, so try a hand-held vacuum instead. Insecticidal soap sprayed on the undersides of the leaves is also effective on flea beetles. Wireworms can be trapped by putting cut pieces of potatoes or carrots in the soil every five feet or so and then digging the pieces up after a few days. Destroy the worms. When young, Colorado potato beetles can be controlled by applications of *Bacillus thuringiensis* var. *san diego*, a beetle Bt proven effective for flea beetles, as well.

Because many beetle species overwinter in the soil as eggs or adults, crop rotation and fall cleanup are vital. New evidence indicates that beneficial nematodes effectively control most pest beetles—if the nematodes are applied during the beetles' soil-dwelling larval stage. Azadirachtin (the active ingredient in some formulations of neem) is also affective against most immature beetles and can be a feeding deterrent for adults. Polyester row covers, securely fastened to the ground, can provide excellent control for most beetles. Obviously, row covers are of no use if the beetles are in a larval stage and ready to emerge from the soil (under the row cover!) or if the adult beetles are already established on the plants. Row covers work best in combination with crop rotation. Row covers have limited use on plants such as cucumbers, squash, and melons that need bees to pollinate the blooms, as bees can't penetrate the fabric. Japanese beetle populations can also be reduced in several ways: by applying milky-spore, a naturally occurring, slow-working, soil-borne disease that infects the beetle in

its grub stage; by introducing beneficial nematodes; by applying lime to acidic soil to discourage grubs.

Caterpillars (sometimes called loopers or worms) are the immature stage of moths and butterflies. Most pose no problem in our gardens and we encourage them to visit, but a few are a unwelcome in the vegetable garden. The most notorious are the tomato hornworm, beanlooper, cutworm, and the numerous cabbage worms and loopers that chew ragged holes in leaves. Natural controls include birds, wasps, and disease. Encourage birds by providing a birdbath, shelter, and berry-producing shrubs. Tolerate wasp nests if they're not a threat; provide nectar plants for the mini-wasps. Hand-picking is very effective as well. The disease *Bacillus thuringiensis* var. *kurstaki* is available as a spray in a number of formulas; brands include Bt *kurstaki*, Dipel, and Thuricide. When applied, Bt is a bacteria that causes the fairly young caterpillar to starve to death. Bt-k Bait carries the disease; it lures budworms (caterpillars that bore into buds) from the vegetables to the bait. I seldom use Bt in any form, as it also kills all butterfly and harmless moth larvae.

Cutworms are the caterpillar stage of various moth species. Usually found in the soil, cutworms curl into a ball when disturbed. Cutworms are a particular problem when annual vegetable seedlings first appear or when young transplants are set out. They often chew off the stem at the soil line, killing the plant. Control cutworms by encircling young plants with cardboard collars or placing bottomless tin cans around the plant stem; be sure to sink collars 1 inch into the ground. *Bacillus thuringiensis* gives limited control. Trichogramma miniwasps and black ground beetles are among the cutworm's natural enemies. As those natural predators often are not in a new garden, consider introducing them.

Leaf miners, the larvae of small black or black-and-yellow flies, tunnel through leaves, disfiguring them by leaving patches of dead tissue where they feed. They do not burrow into the root. Leaf miners are a particular problem on chard and beets—crops, which can be protected by applying floating row covers early in the season. Leaf miners also can be controlled somewhat by neem or by applying beneficial nematodes.

Mites are among the few arachnids (spiders and their kin) that pose a problem. Mites are so small they are nearly invisible without the aid of a hand lens. They become a problem when they reproduce in great numbers. An indication of serious mite damage is stippling on the leaves in the form of tiny white or yellow spots and sometimes the formation of tiny webs. The major natural predators of pest mites are predatory mites, mite-eating thrips, and syrphid flies.

Mites are most likely to thrive on dusty leaves and in warm weather. Routinely washing foliage and misting sensitive vegetables help control mites. Mites are seldom a serious problem unless heavy-duty pesticides have been used to kill off predatory mites or plants are grown inside the house. To control mite infestation, cut back the plants and stop applying heavy-duty pesticides. The natural prey-predator balance could return. If all else fails, use the neem derivative, Green Light Fruit, Nut, and Vegetable Spray™, or dispose of the plant.

Nematodes are microscopic round worms that inhabit the soil in most of the United States, particularly the Southeast. Most nematode species live on decaying material or prey on other nematodes, insects, or bacteria. A few types are parasitic, attaching themselves to the roots of plants. Edible plants particularly susceptible to nematode damage include beans, melons, lettuce, okra, pepper, squash, tomatoes, eggplant, and some perennial herbs. The symptoms of nematode damage are stunted-looking plants and small swellings or lesions on the roots.

To control nematodes, rotate annual vegetables with less-susceptible varieties; plant contaminated beds with a blanket of marigolds for a whole season or plant marigolds among your vegetables; keep soil high in organic matter to encourage fungi and predatory nematodes that act as biological controls; if all else fails, grow edibles in sterilized soil in containers.

Snails and **slugs** are not insects, of course, but mollusks. They are especially fond of vegetable greens and seedlings. They feed at night and can go dormant for months in times of stress. In the absence of effective natural enemies (a few snail eggs are consumed by predatory beetles and earwigs), several snail-control strategies are recommended. Since snails and slugs are most active at night after rain or irrigation, that's a good opportunity to find, hand pick, and destroy them. Only repeated forays provide adequate control. A generous dusting of hardwood ashes around susceptible plants gives some control. A copper strip attached to the top perimeter of a planter box effectively repels slugs and snails; the mollusks get a shock when touching the copper. A word of warning: any overhanging leaves that can act as a bridge into the planting bed will defeat the barrier.

Whiteflies are sometimes a problem in mild-winter areas of the country, as well as in greenhouses nationwide. Lettuces, tomatoes, and cucumbers are especially susceptible. Whiteflies can be a persistent problem if plants grow against a building or fence where air circulation is limited. In the garden, Encarsia wasps and other parasitoids usually provide adequate whitefly control. Occasionally, especially in cool weather or in greenhouses, whitefly populations may cause serious plant damage—wilting, slowed growth, delayed flowering. Look under the leaves to determine whether the scalelike, immobile larvae—the young crawling stage—or the pupae are evident in large numbers. If so, wash them off with water from the hose. Repeat the washing three days in a row. In addition, try removing the adults with a hand-held vacuum early in the day when the weather is cool and the flies are less active. Insecticidal soap sprays are quite effective as well.

Wildlife Problems

Rabbits and mice can cause problems for gardeners. To keep them out, use fine-weave fencing around the vegetable garden. If gophers or moles are a problem, plant large vegetables such as peppers, tomatoes, and squash inside chicken-wire baskets in the ground. Make sure the wire sticks up a foot above the ground so the critters can't reach inside. In severe situations, you might have to line whole beds with chicken wire. Gophers usually need to be trapped. Trapping for moles is less successful, but repellents like MoleMed™ sometimes help.

Rotting lettuce showing snail damage

Cats can help with all rodent problems but they seldom provide adequate control. Small, portable electric fences help keep racoons, squirrels, and woodchucks out of the garden. Small-diameter wire mesh, bent into boxes and anchored with ground staples, protects seedlings from squirrels and chipmunks.

Deer are a serious problem—they love vegetables. I've tried myriad repellents, but they gave only short-term control. In some areas deer cause such severe problems that edible plants can't be grown without tall electric or nine-foot fences and/or an aggressive dog. The exception is herbs; deer don't feed on most culinary herbs.

Songbirds, starlings, and crows can be major pests of young seedlings, particularly lettuce, corn, and peas. Cover emerging plants with bird netting firmly anchored to the ground so birds can't get under it and feast.

Pest Controls

Insecticidal soap sprays are effective against many pest insects, including caterpillars, aphids, mites, and whiteflies. They can be purchased or homemade. As a rule, I recommend purchasing insecticidal soaps, as they have been carefully formulated to give the most effective control and are less apt to burn your vegetables. If you make your own, use a mild, liquid dishwashing soap not a caustic detergent.

Neem-based pesticide and fungicide products, which are derived from the neem tree *(Azadirachta indica)*, have relatively low toxicity for mammals but are effective against a wide range of insects. Neem products are considered "organic" pesticides by some organizations but not by others. Products containing a derivative of neem—azadirachtin—are effective because azadirachtin is an insect growth regulator that negatively affects the growth of insects in their immature stages. Sprayed with neem, young leaf miners, cucumber beetles, and aphids don't reach adulthood. BioNeem and Azatin are commercial pesticides containing azadirachtin. Another neem product, Green Light Fruit, Nut, and Vegetable Spray, contains clarified hydrophobic extract of neem oil and is affective against mites, aphids, and some fungus diseases. Neem products are still fairly new in the United States. Although at first neem was thought to be harmless to beneficial insects, recent studies show that some parasitoid beneficial insects that feed on neem-treated insects didn't survive to adulthood.

Pyrethrum, a botanical insecticide, is toxic to a wide range of insects but has relatively low toxicity for most mammals. Pyrethrum also breaks down quickly. The active ingredients are pyrethrins derived from chrysanthemum flowers. Do not confuse pyrethrum with pyrethroids, which are much more toxic synthetics that do not biodegrade as quickly. Many pyrethrums have the synergist piperonyl butoxide (PBO) added to increase the effectiveness. As there is evidence that PBO may affect the human nervous system, try to use pyrethrums without PBO. Wear gloves, goggles, and a respirator when using pyrethrum.

Diseases

Plant diseases are potentially far more damaging to vegetables than are most insects. There are two types of diseases: those caused by nutrient deficiencies and those caused by pathogens. Diseases caused by pathogens, such as root rots, are difficult to control once they begin. Therefore, most plant disease control strategies feature prevention rather than cure.

To keep diseases under control, it is very important to plant the "right plant in the right place." For instance, salad greens in poorly drained soil often develop root rot. Tomatoes planted against a wall are prone

to whiteflies and fungal diseases. Check a plant's cultural needs of before placing it in your garden. Proper light, air circulation, temperature, fertilization, and moisture are important factors in disease control. Finally, whenever possible, choose disease-resistant varieties when a particular pathogen is present or when conditions are optimal for the disease. The entries for individual plants in "The Rainbow Vegetable Encyclopedia" give specific cultural and variety information. As a final note, plants infected with disease pathogens should always be discarded, never composted.

Nutritional Deficiencies

For additional basic information on plant nutrients, see the soil preparation information given in Appendix A on page 91. As with pathogens, the best way to solve nutritional problems is to prevent them. While vegetables can suffer from mineral deficiencies (most often caused by a pH below 6 or above 7.5), the most common nutritional deficiency is lack of nitrogen. Vegetables demand fairly high amounts of nitrogen to grow vigorously. Nitrogen deficiency is especially prevalent in sandy soil or soil low in organic matter. (Although clay and organic matter provide little nitrogen, they do hold on to it, however, making nitrogen available to plant roots and keeping it from leaching.)

The main symptom of nitrogen deficiency is a pale, slightly yellow cast to the foliage, especially the lower, older leaves. For quick-growing crops like baby lettuces, by the time the symptoms show, it's too late to apply a cure. You might as well pull out the plants and salvage what you can. To prevent the problem from recurring, supplement vegetable beds with a good source of organic nitrogen like blood meal, chicken manure, and fish emulsion. For most vegetables—as they are going to be growing for a long season—correct the nitrogen deficiency by applying fish emulsion according to the directions on the container; reapply in a month or so. Usually nitrogen does not stay in the soil for more than four to six weeks; it leaches into the ground water.

While I've stressed nitrogen deficiency, the real trick is to achieve a good nitrogen balance in your soil. Although plants must have nitrogen to grow, too much nitrogen causes leaf edges to die, promotes succulent

new growth savored by aphids, and makes plants prone to cold damage.

Diseases Caused by Pathogens

Anthracnose is a fungal problem primarily in the eastern United States on beans, tomatoes, cucumbers, and melons. Affected plants develop spots on the leaves. Furthermore, beans develop sunken black spots on their pods and stems; melons, cucumbers, and tomatoes develop sunken spots on their fruits. Anthracnose spreads readily in wet weather and overwinters on debris in the soil. Crop rotation, good air circulation, and choosing resistant varieties are the best defenses. Neem-based Green Light Fruit, Nut, and Vegetable Spray™ gives some control.

Blights and **bacterial diseases** include a number of diseases caused by fungi and bacteria that affect vegetables, and their names hint at the damage they do—such as blights, wilts, and leaf spots. As a rule, they are more of a problem in rainy and humid areas. Given the right conditions, they can be a problem in most of North America. Early blight strikes tomatoes when plants are in full production or under stress and causes dark brown spots with rings in them on older leaves, which then turn yellow and die. Potato tubers also are prone to early blight; they become covered with corky spots. Warm, moist conditions promote the disease. Late blight causes irregular gray spots on the tops of tomato leaves and white mold on the spots on the undersides of leaves. Leaves eventually turn brown and dry looking. Fruits develop water-soaked spots that eventually turn corky. Potato tubers develop spots that eventually lead to rot. Cool nights with warm days in wet weather are ideal conditions for the disease. Halo and common blight cause spots on the leaves and pods of most types of beans and are most active in wet weather. All these blight-causing fungi and bacteria overwinter on infected plant debris. To prevent infections, avoid overhead watering, clean up plant debris in the fall, rotate crops, and purchase only certified disease-free seed potatoes. Bacterial wilt affects cucumbers, melons, and sometimes squash. Spread by cucumber beetles, bacterial wilt causes plants to wilt and eventually die. To diagnose the disease, cut a wilted stem and look for milky sap that forms a thread when the tip of a stick touches it and is drawn away. The disease overwinters in cucumber beetles; installing floating row covers over young plants are the best defenses.

Damping off occurs when a parasitic fungus living near the soil surface attacks young plants in their early seedling stage. It causes seedlings to wilt and rot at the point where they emerge from the soil. This fungus thrives under dark, humid conditions. It often can be thwarted by growing seedlings in a bright, well-ventilated place in fast-draining soil. Whenever possible, start seedlings in sterilized soil.

Fusarium wilt is a soil-borne fungus most prevalent in the warm parts of the country. It causes an overall wilting of the plant; leaf stems droop and the lower and outer leaves turn yellow, then brown, before the plant dies. Plants most susceptible to different strains of fusarium wilt include tomatoes, potatoes, peppers, cucumber, squash, melons, peas, asparagus, and basil. Although a serious problem in some areas, fusarium wilt can only be controlled by planting resistant varieties. Crop rotation is also helpful.

Mildews are fungal diseases which under certain conditions affect some vegetables—particularly peas, spinach, and squash. There are two types of mildews: powdery and downy. Powdery mildew appears as a white, powdery dust on a leaf surface; downy mildew makes velvety or fuzzy white, yellow, or purple patches on leaves, buds, and tender stems. The poorer the air circulation and the more humid the weather, the more apt your plants are to have downy mildew.

To control both mildews, make sure plants have plenty of sun and are not crowded by other vegetation. If you must use overhead watering, do so in the morning. In some cases, powdery mildew can be washed off the plant. Do so early in the day, so that the plant has time to dry before evening. Powdery mildew is almost always visible on squash and pea plants at the end of the season; that's not a problem as the vegetables have usually stopped producing by then.

Research at Cornell University has proven that lightweight "summer" horticultural oil combined with baking soda is effective against powdery mildew on some plants. Combine 1 tablespoon of baking soda and 2 $\frac{1}{2}$ teaspoons of summer oil with 1 gallon of water. Spray weekly. Test on a small part of the plant first. Don't use horticultural oil on very hot days or on plants that are moisture stressed. After applying the oil, wait at least a month before using any sulfur sprays on the same plant.

You can make a tea for combating powdery mildew and possibly other disease-causing fungi by wrapping a gallon of well-aged, manure-based compost in burlap then steeping the compost in a 5-gallon bucket of water for about three days in a warm place. Spray the tea on plants every three to four days, in the evening if possible, until symptoms disappear.

Downy mildew is sometimes a problem on lettuces, especially in late fall, in cold frames, and under row covers. So select resistant varieties when possible; try to keep irrigation water off the leaves; prevent plants from crowding; and dispose of all infected leaves and plants. When growing greens in a cold frame, make sure the air circulation is optimal.

Root rots and **crown rots** are caused by a number of different fungi. The classic symptom of root rot is wilting—even when a plant is well-watered. Sometimes one side of the plant will wilt; more often the whole plant wilts. Affected plants are often stunted and yellow as well. The diagnosis is complete when the dead plant is pulled up to reveal rotten, black roots. Crown rot, primarily a problem in the Northeast, is a fungus that kills plants at the crown. Root and crown rots are most often caused by poor drainage; there is no cure when they involve the whole plant. Remove and destroy the plants and correct the drainage problem.

Verticillium wilt is a soil-borne fungus that can be a problem in most of North America, especially the cooler sections. The symptom of verticillium wilt is a sudden wilting of one part of or all of the plant. If you continually lose tomatoes or eggplants, this or one of the other wilts could be the problem. There is no cure. If this fungus is in your soil, plant resistant species or varieties.

Viruses attack a number of plants. Symptoms are stunted growth and deformed or mottled leaves. The mosaic viruses destroy chlorophyll in the leaves, causing them to become yellow and blotched in a mosaic pattern. There is no cure for viral conditions, so the affected plants must be destroyed. Tomatoes, cucumbers, and beans are particularly susceptible. Viral diseases can be transmitted by aphids and leaf hoppers or by seeds. So seed savers should be extra careful to learn the symptoms in individual plant species. Use resistant varieties when they're available.

resources

Gardening and Cooking Supplies

Gardener's Supply Company
128 Intervale Road
Burlington, VT 05401
Extensive collection of gardening tools and supplies

Native Seeds/SEARCH
526 North 4th Avenue
Tucson, AZ 85705
Membership: 20.00
Low income/student: $12.00
Catalog: $1.00 for nonmembers
Fascinating selection of foodstuffs, including red and blue cornmeals, beans, chile products

The Natural Gardening Company
217 San Anselmo Avenue
San Anselmo, CA 94960
Gardening supplies, organic fertilizers, beneficial nematodes

Nutrite Inc.
P.O. Box 160
Elmira, Ontario
Canada N3B 2Z6
Canadian source of gardening supplies

Peaceful Valley Farm Supply
P.O. Box 2209
Grass Valley, CA 95945
Gardening supplies, organic fertilizers, seeds for cover crops

Sur La Table
Catalog Division
1765 Sixth Avenue South
Seattle, WA 98134
Cooking equipment

Williams-Sonoma
Mail Order Department
P.O. Box 7456
San Francisco, CA 94120-7456
Cooking equipment and specialty foods

Wycliffe Gardens
P.O. Box 430
Kimberly, British Columbia
Canada BC V1A 2Y9
Canadian source of gardening supplies

Seeds and Plants

Abundant Life Seed Foundation
P.O. Box 772
Port Townsend, WA 98368
Non-profit organization
Membership: $30.00; Limited income: $20.00
Catalog: $2.00 donation for nonmembers
Various open-pollinated, multi-colored heirlooms

Becker's Seed Potatoes
R.R. 1
Trout Creek, Ontario
Canada P0H 2L0
Certified seed potatoes including 'All Red' and 'All Blue'

Bountiful Gardens
18001 Shafer Ranch Road
Willits, CA 95490-9626
Main Catalog: free in United States; $2.00 elsewhere
Rare seeds catalog: $2.00
Interesting selection of open-pollinated varieties; organic gardening supplies

W. Atlee Burpee & Co.
Warminster, PA 18974
Wide variety of types of seed

Chiltern Seeds
Bortree Stile
Ulverston
Cumbria LA12 7PB England
Wide selection of seeds including unusual and colorful vegetables

The Cook's Garden
P.O. Box 535
Londonderry, VT 05148
Great selection of colorful, tasty vegetable varieties; also herb and flower seeds

DeGiorgi Company, Inc.
6011 North Street
Omaha, NE 68117-1634
Catalog: $2.00
Variety of vegetables, herbs, and flowers including many colorful varieties

The Digger's Club
Heronswood, 105 Latrobe Parade
Dromana 3936
Australia
Seed-exchange club and mail-order catalog with many heirloom varieties

Evergreen Y. H. Enterprises
P.O. Box 17538
Anaheim, CA 92817
Catalog: $2.00 United States; $2.50 Canada
*Oriental vegetables and herbs including
unusual and colorful amaranths and radishes*

Fox Hollow Seeds
P.O. Box 148
McGrann, PA 16236
Catalog: $1.00
*Specializes in heirloom herbs, vegetables, and
flowers including hard-to-find, colorful veg-
etable varieties*

Garden City Seeds
778 Highway 93 North
Hamilton, MT 59840
*Colorful varieties rich in healthy phytonutri-
ents; specializes in varieties for short seasons
and cold climates*

The Gourmet Gardener
8650 College Boulevard
Overland Park, KS 66210
*Vegetables, herbs, edible flowers; some heir-
looms, many colorful varieties*

Gurney Seed & Nursery Company
110 Capital Street
Yankton, SD 57079
*Wide variety of seeds and plants including pur-
ple asparagus*

Harris Seeds and Nursery
P.O. Box 22960
Rochester, NY 14692
Carries many heirloom seeds

J. L. Hudson, Seedsman
Star Route 2, Box 337
La Honda, CA 94020
For catalog: P.O. Box 1058, Redwood City,
CA 94064
Catalog: $1.00
Open-pollinated; heirlooms; unusual varieties

Johnny's Selected Seeds
Foss Hill Road
Albion, ME 04910-9731
*Excellent selection of herb and vegetable seeds;
many unusual and colorful varieties*

Landis Valley
Heirloom Seed Project
2451 Kissel Hill Road
Lancaster, PA 17601

Catalog $4.00
Heirloom vegetable seeds and flowers

Lockhart Seeds, Inc.
P.O. Box 1361
3 North Wilson Way
Stockton, CA 95205
*Mostly commercial varieties with an especially
large selection of onion varieties*

Native Seeds/SEARCH
526 North 4th Avenue
Tucson, AZ 85705
Membership: $20.00; Low-income/student:
$12.00
Catalog: $1.00 for nonmembers
*Great selection of amaranth and colorful corn.
Nonprofit organization dedicated to preservation of traditional crops, seeds, and farming
methods of the native peoples of the southwest-
ern United States and northern Mexico.
Membership includes quarterly newsletter, catalog, and 10 percent discount on items in the
catalog and the retail store in Tucson.*

Nichols Garden Nursery
1190 North Pacific Highway NE
Albany, OR 97321-4580
*Vegetables and herbs; wide selection of inter-
esting colorful varieties including heirlooms
and European varieties*

Park Seed Company
One Parkton Avenue
Greenwood, SC 29647
Wide variety of vegetables, herbs, and flowers

The Pepper Gal
P.O. Box 23006
Ft. Lauderdale, FL 33307-3006
Catalog: $2.00
*Great selection of hot, sweet, and ornamental
peppers*

Pinetree Garden Seeds
Box 300
New Gloucester, ME 04260
*Good selection of heirloom, European, and
open-pollinated varieties*

Plants of the Southwest
Agua Fria, Route 6, Box 11A
Santa Fe, NM 87501
Catalog: $3.50
*Open-pollinated seeds of warm-season vegeta-
bles, heirlooms, grasses, and wildflowers*

Redwood City Seed Company
P.O. Box 361
Redwood City, CA 94064
Catalog: $1.00 in United States, Canada,
Mexico; $2.00 in other countries
*Specializes in endangered cultivated plants;
carries many unusual vegetable varieties*

Ronniger's Seed & Potato Company
P.O. Box 307
Ellensburg, WA 98926
*Certified organic seed potatoes and certified,
disease-free seed potatoes including colorful
varieties; also red scallions*

Santa Barbara Heirloom Nursery
P.O. Box 4235
Santa Barbara, CA 93140-4235
*Certified, organically grown, heirloom
seedlings including colorful pepper, eggplant,
and tomato seedlings. Offers a rainbow tomato
collection of six different colored tomatoes*

Seeds Blüm
HC 33 Box 2057
Boise, ID 83706
Catalog: $3.00; First Class option: $5.00
*A leader in the field, offering unusual and col-
orful vegetable varieties for years*

Seeds of Change
P.O. Box 15700
Santa Fe, NM 87506-5700
Organically grown vegetable and herb seeds

Seed Savers Exchange
3076 North Winn Road
Decorah, IA 52101
Membership fee: $25.00
Low-income/Senior/Student: $20.00
Canadian: $30.00; Overseas: $40.00
Catalog for purchasing selected seeds is free
to nonmembers and members.
*Nonprofit organization dedicated to saving
vegetable gene pool diversity. The only source
for many rare and heirloom vegetable seeds.
Members join an extensive network of garden-
ers saving and exchanging seeds.*

Shepherd's Garden Seeds
30 Irene Street
Torrington, CT 06790-6658
*Many European vegetable varieties, some of
unusual colors; also herbs and flowers*

Jackson, NJ 08527-0308
Wide variety of types of seeds

Thompson & Morgan, Ltd.
Poplar Lane
Ipswich
Suffolk 1P8 3BU
England
Wide variety of types of seeds

Tomato Growers Supply Company
P.O. Box 2237
Fort Meyers, FL 33902
Extensive selection of types and colors of tomatoes and peppers

Totally Tomatoes
P.O. Box 1626
Augusta, GA 30903
Extensive selection of types and colors of tomatoes and peppers

Vermont Bean Seed Company
Garden Lane
Fair Haven, VT 05743
Extensive selection of many types of beans as well as other vegetables

Wood Prairie Farm
49 Kinney Road
Bridgewater, ME 04735
Certified, organic seed potatoes and other organic vegetables; grains for cooking including Mandan Bride cornmeal and different colored popcorns

Non-Mail Order Source

Look for seeds by Renee's Garden in your local retail outlets. Renee's Garden offers an excellent selection of colorful, high-quality vegetable varieties. Call 1-888-880-7228 for more information.

R. H. Shumway's
P.O. Box 1
Graniteville, SC 29829-0001
Wide variety of seeds including many heirlooms; also bare-root purple asparagus

Southern Exposure Seed Exchange
P.O. Box 170
Earlysville, VA 22936
Catalog: $2.00
Carries many open-pollinated and heirloom varieties and a good selection of colorful vegetables; specializes in heat-tolerant varieties

Stokes Seeds, Inc.
P.O. Box 548
Buffalo, NY 14240
Wide variety of vegetables, herbs, and flowers

Territorial Seed Company
P.O. Box 157
Cottage Grove, OR 97424-0061
Good selection of heirloom and other open-pollinated varieties; several colorful varieties

Thompson & Morgan Inc.
P.O. Box 1308

Bibliography

Bender, Steve, ed. *Southern Living Garden Book*. Birmingham, Alabama: Oxmoor House, 1998.

Bubel, Nancy. *The New Seed-Starters Handbook*. Emmaus, Pa.: Rodale Press, 1988.

Carr, Anna. *Rodale's Color Handbook of Garden Insects*. Emmaus, Pa.: Rodale Press, 1979.

Cathey, H. Marc. *Heat-Zone Gardening. How to Choose Plants That Thrive in Your Region's Warmest Weather*. Alexandra, Va.: Time-Life Custom Publishing, 1998.

Cool, Jesse Ziff. *Tomatoes: A Country Garden Cook Book*. San Francisco: Collins Publishers, 1994.

Creasy, Rosalind. *Blue Potatoes, Orange Tomatoes*. San Francisco: Sierra Club Books for Children, 1994.

Creasy, Rosalind. *The Complete Book of Edible Landscaping*. San Francisco: Sierra Club Books, 1982.

Cutler, Karan Davis. *Burpee: The Complete Vegetable and Herb Gardener: A Guide to Growing Your Garden Organically*. New York: Macmillan Incorporated, 1997.

Editors of Sunset Books and Sunset Magazine. *Sunset National Garden Book*. Menlo Park, Calif.: Sunset Books, 1997.

Editors of Sunset Books and Sunset Magazine. *Sunset Western Garden Book*. Menlo Park, Calif.: Sunset Publishing Corporation, 1995.

Faccaiola, Stephen. *Cornucopia: A Source Book for Edible Plants*. Vista, Calif.: Kampong Publications, 1990.

Gilkeson, Linda, Pam Peirce, and Miranda Smith. *Rodale's Pest & Disease Problem Solver: A Chemical-Free Guide to Keeping Your Garden Healthy*. Emmaus, Pa.: Rodale Press, 1996.

Madison, Deborah. *Vegetarian Cooking for Everyone*. New York: Broadway Books, 1997.

McFadden, Christine, with Kathleen Zelman. *The Harvest of Healing Foods: Recipes and Remedies for the Mind, Body, and Soul*. Lincolnwood, Ill.: Contemporary Books, 1998.

McGee, Harold. *On Food and Cooking: The Science and Lore of the Kitchen*. New York: Charles Scribner's Sons, 1996.

Ogden, Shepherd. *Step by Step Organic Vegetable Gardening: The Gardening Classic Revised and Updated*. New York: HarperCollins, 1992.

Olkowski, William, Sheila Daar, and Helga Olkowski. *The Gardener's Guide to Common-Sense Pest Control*. Newtown, Conn.: Taunton Press, 1995.

Patent, Dorothy Hinshaw and Diane E. Bilderback. *The Harrowsmith Country Life Book of Garden Secrets*. Charlotte, Vt.: Camden House Publishing, Inc., 1991.

Ravens, Peter H., Ray F. Evert, and Susan E. Eichhorn. *Biology of Plants,* Sixth Edition. New York: W. H. Freeman and Company, 1999.

Reilly, Ann. *Park's Success with Seeds*. Greenwood, S.C.: Geo. W. Park Seed Co., 1978.

Ronzio, Robert A., Ph.D. *The Encyclopedia of Nutrition and Good Health*. New York: Facts on File, Inc., 1997.

Rupp, Rebecca. *Blue Corn and Square Tomatoes: Unusual Facts about Common Garden Vegetables*. Pownal, Vt.: Storey Communications, Inc., 1987.

Shepherd, Renee. *Recipes from a Kitchen Garden*. Felton, Calif.: Shepherd's Garden Publishing, 1987.

Shepherd, Renee, and Fran Raboff. *Recipes from a Kitchen Garden, Volume II*. Felton, Calif.: Shepherd's Garden Publishing, 1991.

Schneider, Elizabeth. *Uncommon Fruits and Vegetables: A Common Sense Guide*. New York: Harper & Row, Publishers, 1986.

Stickland, Sue. *Heirloom Vegetables—Home Gardener's Guide to Finding and Growing Vegetables from the Past*. London: Gaia Books Limited, 1998.

Troetschler, Ruth, Alison Woodworth, Sonja Wilcomer, Janet Hoffmann, and Mary Allen. *Rebugging Your Home & Garden: A Step by Step Guide to Modern Pest Control*. Los Altos, Calif.: PTF Press, 1996.

Watson, Benjamin. *Taylor's Guide to Heirloom Vegetables*. Boston: Houghton Mifflin Company, 1996.

Weaver, William W. *Heirloom Vegetable Gardening: A Master Gardener's Guide to Planting, Seed Saving, and Cultural History*. New York: Henry Holt and Company, 1996.

Whealy, Kent, editor. *The Garden Seed Inventory,* 5th edition. Decorah, Iowa: Seed Savers Exchange, 1999.

Magazines

The Magazine for Food and Health: Eating Well. Telemedia Publishing, New York. For subscriptions: P.O. Box 54263, Boulder, CO 80323.

Other Resources

American Horticulture Society. "Plant Heat-Zone Map." 1-800-777-7931, Extension 45. Cost: $15.00.

acknowledgments

My garden is the foundation for my books, photography, and recipes. For nearly twelve months of the year we toil to keep it beautiful and bountiful. Unlike most gardens, it is a photo studio and trial plot, and must therefore be glorious, healthy, and productive. To complicate the maintenance, all the beds are changed at least twice a year. Needless to say, it is a large undertaking. For two decades, a quartet of talented organic gardener/cooks have not only given it hundreds of hours of loving attention, but they have also been generous with their vast knowledge of plants. Together we have forged our concept of gardening and cooking, much of which I share with you in this series of garden cookbooks.

I wish to thank Wendy Krupnick for giving the garden such a strong foundation and Joe Queirolo for maintaining it for many years and lending it such a gentle and sure hand. For the last decade, Jody Main and Duncan Minalga have helped me expand my garden horizons. No matter how complex the project, they enthusiastically rise to the occasion. In the kitchen, I am most fortunate to have Gudi Riter, a very talented cook who developed many of her skills in Germany and France. I thank her for the help she provides as we create recipes and present them in all their glory. I want to thank Carole Saville who, over the years, has generously shared her vast knowledge of unusual plants and exotic cooking techniques.

I thank Dayna Lane for her steady hand and editorial assistance. In addition to day-to-day compilations, she joins me on our constant search for the most effective organic pest controls, superior vegetable varieties, and the best sources for plants.

I rely on technical support from an assortment of people in a number of fields. Nona Koivula, executive Director of All-American Selection, leads me to knowledgeable experts and locates photos of unusual vegetables; John Navazio Ph.D, plant breeder at Alf Christianson Seed Co., provides nutritional information; Richard Merrill, botany professor extrodinaire at Cabrillo College, lends botanical support; and W. Atlee Burpee Co. and Park Seeds, provide needed photos.

I would also like to thank a large supporting cast: my husband, Robert, who gives such quality technical advice and loving support; Jan Blüm, of Seeds Blüm and Renee Shepherd of Renee's Garden for sharing years of "rainbow" information; Doug Gosling, for his love of exotic vegetables; a triumvirate including Jane Whitfield, Linda Gunnarson, and David Humphrey who were integral to the initial vision of this book; Kathryn Sky-Peck for providing the design and quality of the layout; and Marcy Hawthorne for the lovely drawings. Heartfelt thanks to Eric Oey and to the entire Periplus staff, especially Deane Norton, Jan Johnson, and Sonia MacNeil, for their help. Finally, I would like to thank my editor, Jeanine Caunt, for her attention to detail and her enthusiasm. Her constant vigilance assures a book of which we can all be proud.